Rose Always

A Love Story

Rose Always

A Love Story

Poems

Maja Trochimczyk

Moonrise Press

Copyright Page

Rose Always – A Love Story by Maja Trochimczyk

Published by Moonrise Press
P.O. Box 4288, Los Angeles – Sunland, CA 91041-4288
www.moonrisepress.com; info@moonrisepress.com

Poetry and photos © Copyright 2008-2020 by Maja Trochimczyk
This edition is to replace all previous versions of *Rose Always –
A Court Love Story*. It adds new poems, in different sections, and
deletes all "court"-related quasi-non-fiction prose fragments.

Printed in the United Stated of America

All Rights Reserved 2020 by Moonrise Press
Rose photographs © 2008-2019 by Maja Trochimczyk

Book design and layout by Maja Trochimczyk using fonts:
Monotype Corsiva and Stencil (title pages),
Garamond and Century (poems)

The Library of Congress Publication Data:
Trochimczyk, Maja, 1957–
[Poems. English. Collections by a single author]
Rose Always – A Love Story / Maja Trochimczyk
224 pp. (xiv and 210 pages); size 15.2 x 22.9 cm.
Includes 94 color photos, 7 color title pages and one portrait.

ISBN 978-1-945938-17-7 (color paperback)
ISBN 978-1-945938-48-1 (color hardcover)
ISBN 978-1-945938-18-4 (E-book in E-Pub format)

10 9 8 7 6 5 4 3 2 1

*~ for the Love of my Life
surprising, but not really*

Table of Contents

Preface
Acknowledgments
Prior Publication Credits

Rose Always

I. Wishing — Annunciatio   1

Prelude	≈♥≈	3
Longing	≈♥≈	4
Love Diamond	≈♥≈	5
Escape	≈♥≈	6
Bluebird	≈♥≈	7
Infinity	≈♥≈	8

II. Seeing — Revelatio   9

In the Desert	≈♥≈	10
At Noon	≈♥≈	11
Dog Story	≈♥≈	12
Laundry Day	≈♥≈	13
A Desert Walk	≈♥≈	14
Cry Me a River	≈♥≈	15
Presence	≈♥≈	16
Oasis	≈♥≈	17
The Still Point	≈♥≈	18
Narrow Path	≈♥≈	19
Dirt Bike	≈♥≈	20
Chocolate Kiss	≈♥≈	21
Gentleness	≈♥≈	22
Secrets	≈♥≈	23
Smiling	≈♥≈	24
Afterglow	≈♥≈	25
The Arrow	≈♥≈	26
At Sunset	≈♥≈	27
On the Hilltop	≈♥≈	28
A Tale of Magic	≈♥≈	29
Waves	≈♥≈	30
Plato's Trinity	≈♥≈	31

Confession ≈♥≈ 32
Beyond Clouds ≈♥≈ 33
What You Wear ≈♥≈ 34
The Halo ≈♥≈ 35
In Sight ≈♥≈ 36
Novelty ≈♥≈ 37
Shining ≈♥≈ 38
Lucky Charms ≈♥≈ 39
Up, Up, Up ≈♥≈ 40

III. Longing – Separatio   41

Once ≈♥≈ 42
A Vision ≈♥≈ 43
My Man of Mystery ≈♥≈ 45
Moonshine ≈♥≈ 46
Phone Call Away ≈♥≈ 47
The Bluest ≈♥≈ 48
Crystallization ≈♥≈ 49
Magic ≈♥≈ 50
Prayer of the Unseen ≈♥≈ 51
Really ≈♥≈ 52
Indebted ≈♥≈ 53
Within ≈♥≈ 54
Philadelphia ≈♥≈ 55
Eagle Rock ≈♥≈ 56
Closeness ≈♥≈ 58
Clarity ≈♥≈ 59
Planting ≈♥≈ 60
Blessings ≈♥≈ 61
A Dirge ≈♥≈ 62
Radiant ≈♥≈ 63
It's Wonderful ≈♥≈ 64
Night Trees ≈♥≈ 65
By Chance ≈♥≈ 66
"Look at me…" ≈♥≈ 67
Hope ≈♥≈ 68
Tiger Nights ≈♥≈ 69
The Music Box ≈♥≈ 71
Painting ≈♥≈ 73
Ultraviolet ≈♥≈ 74
Revelation ≈♥≈ 75
Song of Gratitude ≈♥≈ 76

IV. Knowing – Communio 77

Turquoise and Gold ≈♥≈ 78
My Quest ≈♥≈ 79
Thanksgiving ≈♥≈ 80
A Portrait in Brackets ≈♥≈ 81
The Other Shore ≈♥≈ 83
Garden of Delight ≈♥≈ 84
Beyond Dark ≈♥≈ 85
Flying ≈♥≈ 86
Forever ≈♥≈ 87
Liquid Grace ≈♥≈ 88
Ella's Voice ≈♥≈ 89
True ≈♥≈ 90
Crescent of Wonder ≈♥≈ 91
Snowfall ≈♥≈ 92
A Snow Valentine ≈♥≈ 93
Da Capo ≈♥≈ 95
The Pearl ≈♥≈ 96
A Letter ≈♥≈ 97
Star Gazing ≈♥≈ 98
Arrival ≈♥≈ 99
Going Home ≈♥≈ 100
Fairy-Tale Queen ≈♥≈ 101
Crowning ≈♥≈ 102
Good, Very Good ≈♥≈ 103
Remember ≈♥≈ 104
Rose Always ≈♥≈ 105

V. Feeling – Consolatio 107

Being ≈♥≈ 108
Hurting ≈♥≈ 109
Awe ≈♥≈ 110
Day by Day ≈♥≈ 111
Troubles ≈♥≈ 112
Most Wanted ≈♥≈ 113
Damage Report ≈♥≈ 113
Ready to Wear ≈♥≈ 115
The Great Beyond ≈♥≈ 116
The Waiting ≈♥≈ 117
Acceptance ≈♥≈ 119
Orion ≈♥≈ 120

Waterfall	≈♥≈	121
In a Winter Garden	≈♥≈	122
Midnight Fire	≈♥≈	123
Chaconne in D Minor	≈♥≈	124
Pining	≈♥≈	125
My Full Moon in September	≈♥≈	126
Foxes	≈♥≈	127
....Around the Roses	≈♥≈	128
Not Aspartame	≈♥≈	129
A Tale of Tomorrow	≈♥≈	130
The Way Out	≈♥≈	131
What's Possible	≈♥≈	132
New Beginning	≈♥≈	133
A Walk in the Canyon	≈♥≈	134
Tiger Dreams	≈♥≈	135
A Ballad of New Heart	≈♥≈	136
A Ballad of New Sun	≈♥≈	138
A Ballad of Golden Scroll	≈♥≈	140
My Gifts	≈♥≈	142
How to Cross the Great White	≈♥≈	143

VI. Loving – Adoratio   145

After the Crossing	≈♥≈	146
Rose Garland	≈♥≈	147
Vortex	≈♥≈	148
Lauda	≈♥≈	149
Rose Window	≈♥≈	150
Future, Past Perfect	≈♥≈	152
Many Happy Returns	≈♥≈	153
Adorable	≈♥≈	154
A Jewel Box Sunrise	≈♥≈	155
Always	≈♥≈	156
Countryside	≈♥≈	157
Landscapes: A Guidebook	≈♥≈	158
Skylark's Lesson	≈♥≈	160
Liquid Honey	≈♥≈	162
Topaz Eyes	≈♥≈	163
Things Not to Say on a Lazy Afternoon	≈♥≈	164
In Case You Did Not Know	≈♥≈	165
How to Domesticate a Cat	≈♥≈	166
Midnight Cat	≈♥≈	168

Sunfire Foxes ≈♥≈ 170

VII. Being – Illuminatio 171

Lost and Found ≈♥≈ 172
Diamond Days in Crystal Gardens ≈♥≈ 173
See the Sea ≈♥≈ 175
Imagine – A Poem of Light ≈♥≈ 176
On Divine Comedy
and Ice-Cream ≈♥≈ 177
Revelation after Il Paradiso ≈♥≈ 179
Gold, Inside ≈♥≈ 180
Sweet Nothings ≈♥≈ 181
An Invitation to the Dance ≈♥≈ 182
I Did Not Dare to Hope ≈♥≈ 183
What I Learned on Friday Morning ≈♥≈ 184
Winter Solstice ≈♥≈ 186
Midnight Sun ≈♥≈ 188
High Noon ≈♥≈ 189
Just to Make it Clear ≈♥≈ 190
Last Pomegranate ≈♥≈ 191
My Birthday Gift ≈♥≈ 192
Twin Flame Promise ≈♥≈ 194
Late Pomegranates ≈♥≈ 195
In the Valley of Yes ≈♥≈ 196
Land of Milk and Honey ≈♥≈ 197
The Heart ≈♥≈ 198
A Day Trip to Venice ≈♥≈ 199
This Afternoon ≈♥≈ 200
In the Sweet Bye and Bye ≈♥≈ 201
Amber ≈♥≈ 202
Sapphire ≈♥≈ 203
Rainbows ≈♥≈ 204
Diamonds ≈♥≈ 205
Our Champagne Sunday ≈♥≈ 206

Appendix – Music Terms 207
About the Author 208

≈ ♥ ≈

Preface

A book of poetry is a tapestry made with threads of impressions, memories, emotions, images, visions, and dreams. It is made with words borrowed from others and those discovered in moments of revelation. The greatest influence for this collection came from the most astounding and mysterious book of Love that has been written by Life over the course of 15 years. Thank you, my Beloved! Or, as Polish people say, *Kochanie moje...* Our love, compassion, and presence have grown immensely through the turns and twists of our shared Love Story. We have learned the Hawaiian path of "sorry-forgive-thank-love." We traveled through deserts and lush gardens blooming with affection.

I dressed this mystical unending adventure in words, borrowing from the divine poetry of *The Songs of Songs* and its saintly commentators, St. John of the Cross and the blessed Hadewijch. Catholic borrowings also include quotations from the Gospels and allusions to the genres of the litany, lamentation, *collecta, completa, lauda,* the hymn, and the psalm. From the Buddhist and Hindu worlds, the One Divine Love and Light appear along with the concepts of reincarnation, karma, wisdom, compassion, forgiveness, and the mysterious Wheel of Fate that keeps turning, turning, turning... Finally, St. Germain's teachings arise from their hidden depths.

The rose of Antoine de Saint Exupéry's *Little Prince* makes an appearance, and so does the Sleeping Beauty, accompanied by other enchanted figures from antique fairy-tales. Words of my favorite poets – Emily Dickinson, Sappho, Rumi, T.S. Eliot, e.e. cummings, Rainer Maria Rilke, and Czesław Miłosz – are reflected in paraphrases or quotations. Dante's *Il Paradiso,* was an inspiration along with Goethe's *The Sufferings of Young Werther,* Stendhal's *The Red and the Black,* Kant's categorical imperative, Kierkegaard's *Either/Or,* and a variety of country songs, jazz standards, and folk ballads.

Certain poems in this collection have previously appeared in print or online: my chapbooks, *Glorias and Assorted Praises* and *Poems for My Friend* (2007), Poets on Site's chapbooks (2008), *Epiphany Magazine* (2011), *Loch Raven Review* (2010, 2012), *Clockwise Cat* (2015), *Spectrum (2016), Altadena Poetry Review* (2016, 2017), *Into Light* (2016), *Lummox* (2017), many entries of my blog, *Poetry Laurels,* and other venues.

This is the third completely rewritten version of this love story, first published in 2008, revised in 2011, and completely reorganized and expanded in 2020. The two earlier versions have been withdrawn: there was still too much darkness within, that started to lift with the passage of time. Furthermore, the complex format of interlacing poetry and inserts of quasi-non-fiction prose was awkward and distracting from the purity and clarity of the emotional arc of the lyrical narrative.

This book includes most of the poems from previous versions of *Rose Always* (2011). I removed prose fragments that were harming the true, timeless Love Story with its many ups and downs, and a constant focus on the beauty and permanence of True Love. One cannot erase the past, of course, one can only redo the future, and this final version of *Rose Always* is dedicated to the beautiful present, where Love, like the mystical Rose, always is.

~ *Maja Trochimczyk*
July 2020

Acknowledgments

I owe an enormous debt of gratitude to my Muse, who did not quite know what I was doing for many years. Some of his inspired, ardent words are cited here as well. I'm grateful to my dear friends – poets from the Pasadena Poets on Site led by Kathabela Wilson – for their comments and encouragement while I was working on the first version of this book. I read individual poems at Kathabela's Poetry Salon and made many revisions thanks to the advice from Jane Engleman, Sharon Hawley, Deborah P Kolodji, Justin Kibbe, Mina Kirby, Radomir Luza, Mira Mataric, Erica Wilk, and Kathabela. Some poets and friends read through the entire manuscript and provided invaluable insights – Kathabela, Sharon, Jane, Mira, and Elizabeth Kanski. I thank Jane Engleman for inviting me to present an excerpt in a semi-staged reading at the Pasadena Library- Allendale on August 5, 2008 – a turning point where I played my music box, that Lois P. Jones later recorded for my interview on Poets' Café (2011). I acknowledge Dr. Mira Mataric's invitation to be a Featured Poet at the Wright Auditorium, Pasadena Central Library, on September 12, 2008. This reading helped me to refine and focus the first version of book – with prose inserts, that have finally been discarded, since they were detracting from the story-arch of One True Love.

I'm grateful to my three loving children for their patience when I was busy writing, or going to poetry workshops. Ian took sneak peeks at the notebooks and teased me about my future fame and riches as a world-famous poet. Ania persuaded me to start public readings and join poetry groups, while Marcin took care of real life and put a roof over our heads. In over 14 years since starting to write these poems, I have accumulated many more debts of gratitude I cannot quite express. Let me just thank the poet-healers Susan Rogers, Ambika Talwar, and Lois P. Jones, and the talented spiritual healer, Kimberly Meredith. Let me thank Amma with her Sanskrit chants and Eric Raines with his breathing lessons and trauma-clearing sessions. I'd like to express my gratitude to Barbara, Chuck, Jerry, Sherri, and Rosie for their down-to-earth neighborly support. Let me also thank those who taught me the most difficult lessons – of unconditional love and endless forgiveness.

Like J. S. Bach's music, especially *Die Kunst der Fugue* and partitas for solo violin, this collection is written *ad maiorem Dei gloriam*, dedicated to endless brilliance of Divine Light & Love.

~ *Maja Trochimczyk*
Los Angeles, 2008 – 2020

Prior Publication Credits

"Sapphire" in *We Are Here: Village Poets Anthology*, Moonrise Press, 2020.

"This Afternoon," in *Lummox Poetry Anthology*, vol. 9, 2019.

"On Divine Comedy and Ice Cream" in *Grateful Conversations*, Moonrise, 2018.

"Skylark's Lesson," in *Lummox Poetry Anthology*, vol. 8, 2019.

"Winter Solstice," in *Spectrum*, vol. 17, "On Dreams," 2017.

"How to Cross the Great White," "After the Crossing," and "Imagine: A Poem of Light," in *Into Light: Poems and Incantations* (Moonrise Press, 2016).

"An Invitation to the Dance" in *Altadena Poetry Review*, April 2016; reprinted in anthology *Allegro & Adagio: Dance Poems II*, ed. Johnny M. Tucker, Jr., 2017.

"A Revelation After Il Paradiso" in *Angel City Review*, no. 3, Summer 2016.

"Many Happy Returns" in *Spectrum 3: Love Love Love*, February 2016.

"... Around the Roses," on the *Dead Snakes Blog*, January 2016.

"My Full Moon in September" in *Hometown Pasadena*, September 29, 2015.

"Absence" in *heARTbreak: reimagined* anthology, Los Angeles, September 2015.

"The Waiting," and "On Grief and Loss: A Trilogy" in *Femmwise Cat* (a special issue of the *Clockwise Cat*), March 2015, Part II: 92-96.

"Midnight Fire" in *Dandelion Breeze*, the anthology of Southern California Haiku Study Group, Pasadena, November 2013.

"A Portrait in Brackets" in *The Voice of the Village* 4, no. 6, June 2013.

"Most Wanted" in *Loch Raven Review* 8, no. 4, Winter 2012.

"Rose Always" in *The Voice of the Village* 3, no. 6, June 2012.

"Midnight Fire" and "A Jewel Box Sunrise" in *Poetry and Cookies 2012 Anthology*, Altadena Public Library, April 2012.

"A Jewel Box Sunrise" in *San Gabriel Valley Poetry Quarterly* 52 (winter 2011); reprinted in the anthology *From Benicia with Love*, ed. Don Peery. Benicia, 2013.

"The Crescent of Wonder" ("The Cat and the Crescent") *Voice of the Village*, August 2011; ("A Desert Tale") *San Gabriel Valley Poetry Quarterly* 50, Spring 2011.

"Not Aspartame," in *San Gabriel Valley Poetry Quarterly* 62 (Spring 2014).

"Ready to Wear" in *The Voice of the Village*, 2, no. 4: 25; February 2011.

"Tiger Nights" in the *Epiphany Magazine*, February 2011.

"Rose Window" in *The Voice of the Village* 1, no. 10, August 2010: 27.

"Look at me..." in *Loch Raven Review* 6, no. 1, Spring 2010; reprinted by *Poetry Super Highway*, January 11-18, 2010.

"In a Winter Garden" in *San Gabriel Valley Poetry Quarterly* no. 45 (Spring 2010).

"A Portrait in Brackets (Eidetic Reduction)" in *2010 Calendar of Emerging Urban Poets*, Pasadena, December 2009.

"Snowfall" in the *2009 Emerging Urban Poets Anthology*, Pasadena, November 2009.

77 poems in *Rose Always - A Court Love Story*. Los Angeles: Moonrise Press, 2008, rev. edition, 2011(both versions withdrawn).

"My love is like the weather" *San Gabriel Valley Poetry Quarterly*, 37, Winter 2007.

Many poems were also reprinted on my *Poetry Laurels Blog* and *Chopin with Cherries Blog*, in 2012 to 2020.

Rose Always

A Love Story

Prelude

It all started with love –
a sudden burst of feeling
blinding me to everything
but you

dolcissimo, con amore

It all started in hope –
a shy expectation
that one day you'd come back
and we'd dance

misterioso, con gioia

It all grew in faith –
your faithful presence
making love, our love
possible

pianissimo, con felicità

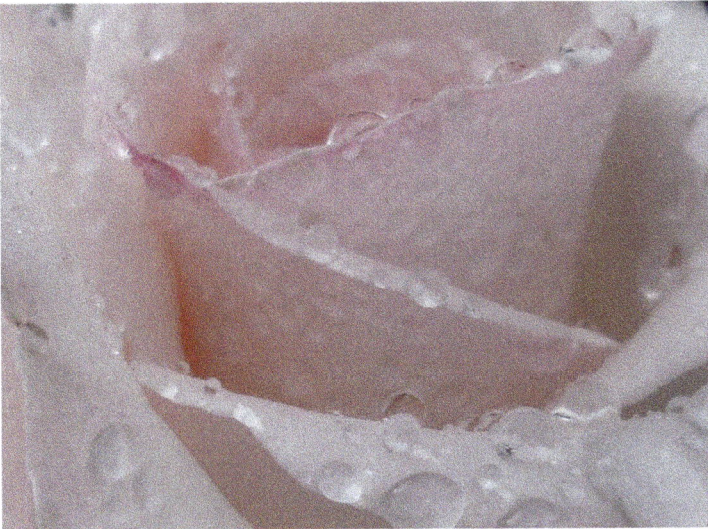

Longing

Fresh, moist petals open
the rose blossoms
in the garden of delight, beauty

She waits for the one
who'd reach past sharp thorns,
past her childish defenses
into her heart

She longs to be touched
and admired for her colors,
for her velvety glow

For the intense burst of pleasure
seducing the one who cares enough
to come with a simple offering –
a life for the rose

Love Diamond

My love is like a sparrow
looking for an oak tree
to rest between its branches

It flutters here and there,
it wanders around,
lost yet happy, it sings

My love is like a sunbeam
shining on the good and ugly,
searching for the crystal reflection
of pure loving – it dreams

My love explodes
like a summer lightning
that leaves hot ashes in its wake,
revealing a diamond of truth

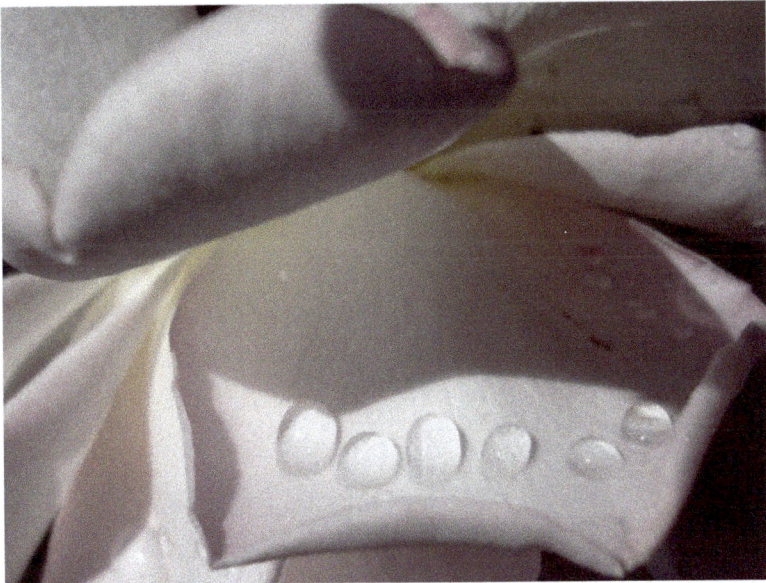

Escape

I cut off all ties with people
live on a desert island

In solitude I admire
the infinite beauty of the world
cracks on the treebark
patterns of rocks near the stream
axial symmetry of dry grasses

I am surrounded by a crystal
dome of freedom

Day by day I come closer
to the end of my path

With one more step
I'll dissolve into the void
that devours

Death has no face
but a thousand hands
reaching out to grab me

No wonder I search for
the way out into the open
where love has gold eyes
and a boyish smile

Only in love, the simplest
deepest, most instinctive
act of Being, I am

Bluebird

I wish I were a bluebird
Outside your window:

I could watch you
working, undisturbed.

I wish I lived in the vastness
of timeless beauty:

Hazel infinity
of your kind eyes.

I wish I could kiss your fingers,
so strong and gentle:

Warm hand resting
on my frightened cheek.

I wish you were my lover
From the Song of Songs:

Our love – a blossom
under almond sky.

Infinity

Up in Heaven
Madonna and her angels
lost patience with my death wish
so, they gave me a gift
for all times –
you

Down on earth
a door opened
to the infinity
of love

On Sunday
I saw the burning flame
from the Song of Songs
beneath your armor
of disaffection

and, as T.S. Eliot said –
all is always now

SEEING

REVELATIO

In the Desert

I found my love in the desert
he is real as rocks in the stream

gentle
as clouds on the mountaintops

strong
as a kiss of sunlight at noon

shy
as the moon in the morning

sweet
 as the taste of mango on my lips

refreshing
as a tangerine

pure
as the baby's breath in my garden

loving
yes, as loving
as I am
when I see him cry

At Noon

"A hug?"
You casually offered
with a shy, knowing smile.

"No, thank you!"
I withdrew,
ashamed of my one wish –

to make time stand still
in the comfort of your arms.

Again –
"Come, let me hug you."

Safe in my garden,
I lost the battle with myself.

Now, I'm tranquil, tender,
still surprised by
the fullness of affection.

Have I thanked you
enough?

Dog Story

My dog ran away
to bring me
the man of my life

a blond one
like my first love
the
with smiley wrinkles
like my last one

(scoundrels both,
as the rest of them)

Are you different?

I cannot tell,
oblivious to all
but your beauty –

Be good, be truthful

Laundry Day

First, I saw your dog
running to me, grinning,
so in love with his mistress

Then, I don't know
what happened,
but you were there

Real, dazzling you,
so attractive
in your dirty T-shirt

I love your bouncy walk,
you look like you dance,
life blessed by sunlight

I'm sorry, I was not ready,
doing laundry in a wet apron,
tired, with messy hair

It does not matter, does it?
When a chance meeting
in my driveway takes us

into timelessness
of ever-present affirmation
"Yes, I do"

A Desert Walk

Your dog welcomes me
with mad displays of affection,
overturning things
with his wildly swinging tail.

He brings the leash in his teeth,
ready for a walk, jumping with excitement.

We go out after sunset,
with my collie – beautiful and scared
of this boisterous stranger,
distrustful of his sudden attachment
to the lady of the house.

The blonde dog cannot be leashed
as he chases each cat, each squirrel.

Yet, he returns quickly, faithfully,
to stay right by my side.

I marvel at his obedience.

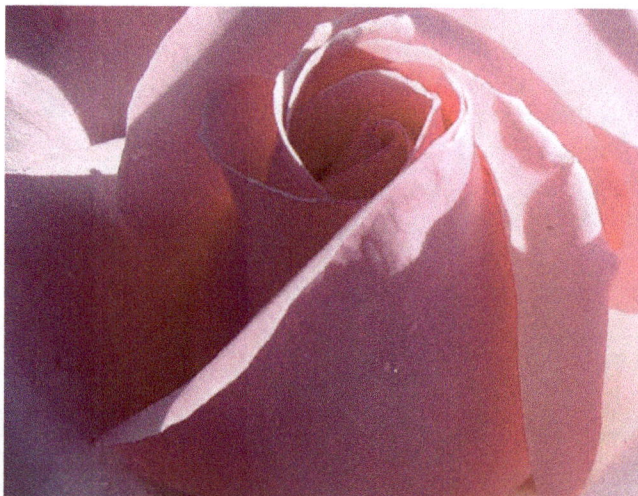

Cry Me a River

You fed my dog.
Now your dog sleeps
in my bedroom,
dreaming of rabbits
in the Wash,
squirrels up the tree.
He surely can climb trees
to catch them in his dreams.

My dreams are different.
I'm the prey, I'm the victim.
I scream with terror.
I wake up with a pounding heart.
Then, I'm sorry to be alive,
for I don't want to –
long overdue
for my date with death.

See? Your dog guards me,
he licks my hands.
He brings me his leash
to play the tug-of-war,
or go to the river
and drown all sorrows
in the Waters of Great Love.

There
I cry and I cry and I cry –

Presence

Half-way through my trip
back in time to before bullets cut my life
into the painful and the disastrous
I rest safely in your presence.

You are here again, anew you laugh
at your dog's antics when he runs towards me,
panting, longing for a pat on the head.

You come when I call you in distress,
exhausted with my day. For a moment
we share the exhilaration of sweet nothings.
For a moment my life makes sense.

Your dog guards me, jumping to lick
my hand at the door, greeting me
like a long-lost lover.

Now I know who you are: the harbinger.
One who carries, who announces. My heart
melts at your sweetest "hello,"
your most charming, "How are you?"

We laugh with an equal mixture of folly
and delight. We find each other
in an oasis of serene certitude
that remains when all else fails.

Oasis

Out of barren flatlands
I came into a place
of tenderness and calm

This oasis was always there
but I could not see it,
hidden in a tangle of worries,
obscured by fear

It happened by chance,
not on purpose

It was your patience
for my dog, I think,
or maybe how you
stretched your arms
to hug me and waited

My next step
wasn't obvious

I had to leave behind
my hurt pride, riches
of aloofness and despair

In my verdant garden
of hibiscus and hummingbirds,
I walked into the music
of your heartbeat
and the day blossomed
with the simplicity of our love

The Still Point

I like the way you look at me,
drinking me in
with quick, short glances,
as if it were too much
to see me whole

Very thirsty for love,
aren't you?

You are the matter of a man
I'm the spirit of a woman,
we belong together

From all the possible futures
I pick the one
where you are with me

The space-time cone moves,
the options shift and shrink
every second

I place you at the still point
of my turning world

Narrow Path

You are my man.
I want no other.
"To have, to hold
To love, to cherish."

I have you now.
You are deep within me.
Forever dancing
in joy of true Being.

On a scale from one to ten
you are one hundred.
One thousand, really,
so much better.

Why do you care
what people think and say?

They'll never change you
from the man of my dreams
back into a stranger.

They will not, but you can
if not careful
on the narrow path
straight into my heart.

Dirt Bike

My beloved
is unlike the others

He knows how
to change my past,
not just my future

I dance with
my Prince Charming

He rides
on a dirt bike,
not a white steed

He wears
mud-splattered leather
not lace – yet, he is true

A man of his word,
truer than a fairy-tale –
so faithful, surprising

Chocolate Kiss

You are my chocolate,
my candy, my lover sweet
in the morning,
alive with kisses

My soul rests
like a bird
on your shoulder

I dream of you
daily

Gentleness

The most perfect being
the most perfect day

Oh, tenderezza

Old ring of sorrow
fell apart in your fingers
Years of misery
crushed into nothing
by your gentle strength

Only the scar remains
deeply cut into the flesh
of my memories
healed by your presence

Everywhere I turn
you are with me

Oh, dolcezza

Brown, smiling eyes
milk chocolate
velvety touch of honey
sweat dripping onto my lips
moist with kisses

Secrets

Your brown eyes shine
with kindness
when you turn your head
to hide your love

Overwhelmed with emotion,
new in such a tough man,
unexpected

You are half-embarrassed,
half-delighted when I speak
of the joy, joy, joy you bring
to brighten my days

Smiling

When you smile
Heaven opens
and the earth grows solid
under my feet,
no longer quicksand –
I breathe slowly

When you smile
pink roses bloom
in my autumn garden,
the pomegranate ripens
in late sunrays –
I fear no one

When you smile
Bach's partita for solo violin
fills the room
with the air of beauty –
angels dance,
I dance with them

Afterglow

you taste of sunlight

sweetness, soft swirls
of ice cream melting
on yellow rays of mango slices
the golden glow of honey
in your eyes

you surprise me
I turn my head and
there you are, looking at me
over your oil-smudged fingers,
engine parts –

smiling

you know what I think
you taste of sunlight

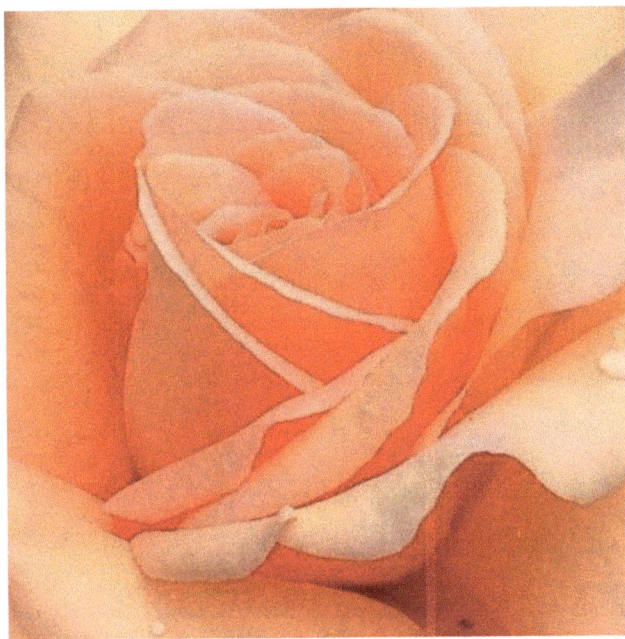

The Arrow

I am drunk on your love
it flows over me in waves

one look

half smile

one caress

The recipe for bliss is simple

you make it with

acceptance

presence

time

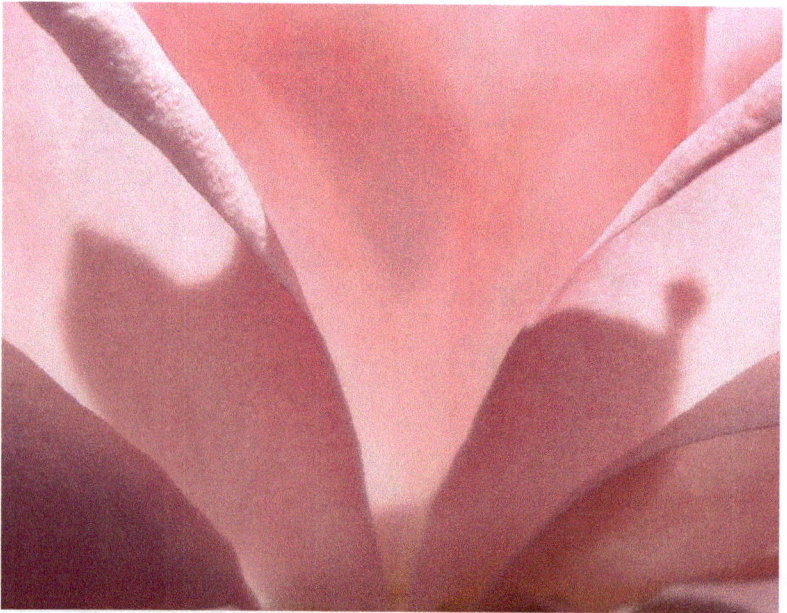

At Sunset

The geometry of shadows
on the hillside
tells me it's five o'clock –

Time for the shadow
on your cheeks
to grow into rough kisses

*   *   *

Crowned with the gold
rays of sunset,
I'm still, full of silence –

Waiting for the earth
to shatter when
your lips touch mine

On the Hilltop

wind kisses me
warmly, gently
like your lips

stars outline
the contours
of your body

darkness covers
my blushing cheeks
with oblivion

A Tale of Magic

Once upon a time
in a far-away land
there was a man
who knew the secret
of loving me

In his hands
my anguish melted
and waned
like distant moon,
while wind played
with my hair
in the mountains

Shocked by acceptance,
I'm no longer sure
I should die
in a month, in a year,
tomorrow

Desire, his desire
healed me

He knew me better
than I knew myself –
what I love,
what I long for

What a gift
to have
for my birthday!

Waves

I wonder if angels
are offended by my hair
glistening in sunlight

Rich waves of wheat
fall onto my shoulders,
wrap me in a smooth coat
waiting to be caressed
by your fingers

Eager to feel your touch,
I don't even cover my head
in prayer – do you think
that the angels mind?

Plato's Trinity

When we met
(ah, the glory of new love!)
you showed me a portrait
of your family – row upon row
solid men and women with weird hairdos.
There, I found you.

How many times
have you shared your life
with a street-walking woman?
In how many gardens
have you rested?

It is all because of Plato,
his trinity of beauty, truth and goodness.
You can blame your eyes,
if you want. Or mine,
so hungry for a trace of affection
in an unfamiliar face,
I thought I knew.

I saw your love – it hit you hard.
It lives in me. It will stay
where it started,
in the torrent
of my words.

Confession

It was as if the sun
walked into the room
when I saw you –

Shining with such,
I don't know, wisdom, maybe,
or knowing me so well

It was the day I did not
feel I should kill myself
not even once

That sunny day you came
and my demons fled
from your brilliance

Like shadows flee
from the merciless
blade of sunrise

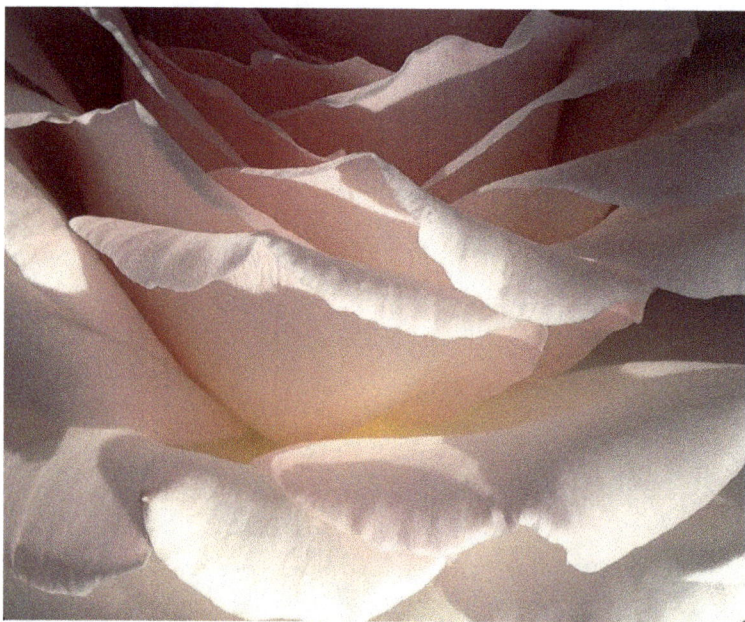

Beyond Clouds

I thought my bucket of happiness
was empty, up in the sky.

I thought it was gone already,
spilled in bitterness

Yet, here you are, smiling
here, caressing my back.

Of the secret of secrets,
I cannot tell.

I found myself in one night
of burning sweetness,

before a gentle kiss
"goodbye"

It was the end, I feared.
You made it real.

Each day – a startling secret.
Each night – a kiss of delight.

I'm bewildered. I'm grateful.

What You Wear

is the garland of my love
and beneath it –

T-shirt and shorts
tank-top and shorts
sweater and shorts

Do you even have real clothes?
You know: suits, dress shirts, and ties
Italian shoes, Swiss watches –
this sort of thing

Funny, I'm always barefoot
when you come –
my rainbow of high heels
abandoned in the closet

In a gray tank top
with a mischievous smile
you are my lifeguard
resting in the sun of our love
under hope's blue sky

You are the perfect man –
a summary of charm, strength
patience, and wisdom –
with dimples and smiley wrinkles
around warm, brown eyes

How on Earth did I find you?
I do not know, but here you are –

A miracle left over from one sad day
healing one broken promise

The Halo

My love is made of gratitude
and sorrow in equal measure –
it thrives in silence
Of thankfulness I build a shield –
smile by smile, day by day

I am sure you did not know
that I made you my guardian angel –
to watch my grief diminish
replaced by *joie de vivre*
born in your presence –

Do the halo and the wings
fit you? They'd better –
you are going to wear them
for a very long time –
till death does us part, no less –

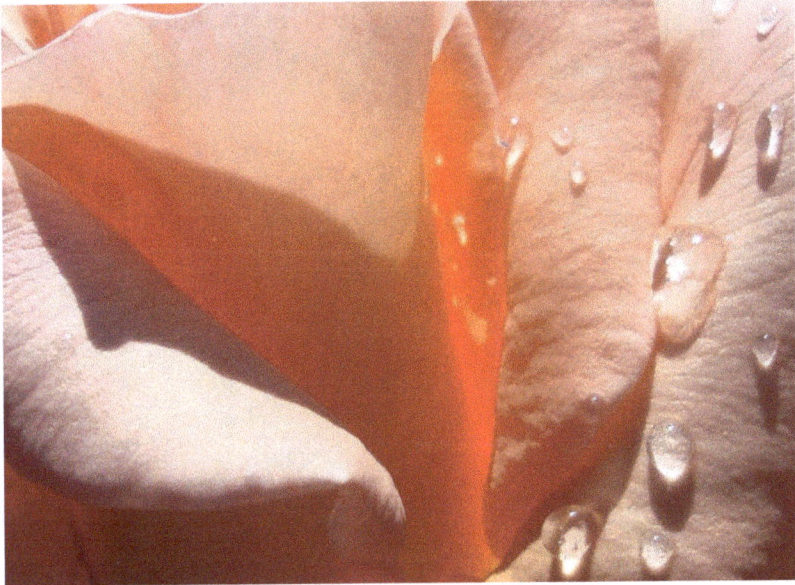

In Sight

My beloved –
you are one in the million
one in the world, really
the one for me

You take me
beyond the beginning
into a country
uniquely of yours
where waves
endlessly crash
on the shore
under the One Love's
gentle whisper

I see infinity
of Divine Light
in your topaz eyes –
The sweetest eyes
that know all sorrows
the happiest eyes
that know me

Novelty

In the newness of this love
we flourish like my pink roses
shining above the lawn's soft blanket

Glorious, resplendent in bright rays
of our Sun, we sing praises
of God's grace in the morning

We are the walnut of perennial wisdom
locked together (two halves in one)
we share one breath of blessed air

Delighted, we peel
minutes off the ancient clock

We keep playing games
of hide and go seek

We win when we grow
more trusting

Shining

What shall I compare you to
in your resplendent beauty?
I already said – "the sun."

Last night I saw Orion – points of light
in the darkness above my house,
a constellation with narrow waist,
broad shoulders – your brilliant double.

The perfect body of an athlete
shines in red clay on a black, ancient vase
in my book of Greek myths –

Full of stories about the whims
of Zeus, hapless Icarus's melting wings,
and poor Semele, burnt to ashes
by her beloved's golden rain.

You hide your beauty in a tattered T-shirt.
You wash the dust off from a desert ride
with your bike buddies. Your radiant smile
entices me to follow you off limits.

What shall I do? What words could capture
the emotion so innocent and pure?
It renders time without you lifeless, pale.

Lucky Charms

Do not try to charm me –
you will not win me over
I'm yours, for I want to

I wished you as my man –
rough, tough and loving
living on edge, in danger

(My mother says I'm dangerous)

I've known you
a month, a week, and a day –
shall I count the minutes?

Time doesn't matter
once we touched
the spring of kindness

once our eyes
revealed one truth
that only lovers know:

a shortcut
through affection
into Being

Up, Up, Up

With you, I'm a fairy-tale princess,
a Cinderella, perhaps, with her gold
spun-glass slipper on my nightstand
by the Polish Bible I use each day
to find out if I've been good.
I really do not know.

Sometimes, I'm a sleeping Beauty
with rosy cheeks, awakened
by the lightest touch of your lips.

Why are you my Prince Charming?
I really do not know. Why
did I have to cross the Great Plains
fly over oceans, wear out
three sets of iron boots, defeat
the Leviathan and the dark
Chameleon in my dreams?

Here I am – here we are
together. Step by step,
holding hands, we climb
the inaccessible heights of God's
white mountain, its snowy peaks
dazzling with the brilliance
of the sky – song – light –

WISHING

ANNUNCIATIO

Once

How gently
did you hold my hand

How tender
was your kiss

That marked
my passage into life
eternal kindness, joy

The angels sang,
blue skies rejoiced

Moon rose –
the crescent of a smile

The shadow passed
tears were no more

You loved me

A Vision

When I opened my desk drawer
your picture was there,
smiling – I'm never without
my lifeguard on the beach.

In a flash, the infinite pierced my eyes.
We come together to the edge
of a giant Light Sphere,
larger than the earth, brighter than the sun,
enormous, beneficent, alive.

We walk into the light,
not seeing where, not looking back
at the path that brought us to the new world.
I take your hand. We are little children
lost in the forest – only there are no trees,
nothing, but eternal brightness,
the silent, loving One who calls us
to come closer, to come together –
the One that is, that waits.

Long ago, I had a vision of myself
in the same light – dazzling and bright,
it bathed me so I'd see how dark I was,
how broken. It flowed around me,
gleaming like a river of white lava –
rich, smooth, opaque,
with the sheen of molten pearls.

One day, I saw the golden halo of divine rays
surrounding the white circle of bread
at Communion. The miniature Sun
shone like a resplendent daisy, blinding
me into humility in the darkness

of the Church – blessed *are*
those who have not seen

Light appears in the riverbed valley
when I walk my dog on Sunday.
The veil lifts. The desert, sand and chaparral
are suffused with glowing presence,
each particle of matter burning from within
with its own white, sparkling, moving flame.

You read about Wisdom
in the Old Book. You know
how She is – incandescent, mobile,
permeating the illusion of matter
with Her luminous rainbow fire.
Ephemeral, these moments burst
through rocks of dead hours.

Rift deepens, time crumbles
in the blaze.

In my incandescent visions,
the world appears as it is –
blossoming in the Divine.
I see us, childlike, together
walking into the light.
What other gifts do I need?

My Man of Mystery

I know everything about you
everything I need –

your beauty, your reckless energy
your focus, your *élan vital* –

seduction of your rakish grin
your affection for the two sons you left –

random pattern of your life
in search of adventure, freedom –

rush of adrenaline in your veins
dirt-bike flying above boulders
desert wind in your face –

craving for the high
of all sensations – magnified –

all pleasure felt – oh, so fully –

I know everything
that's wrong with you –
everything that's right

Only, I cannot figure out
why you had to love me
when you did –

Moonshine

The moon rose without question.
With certitude, it shines upon crickets
counting away last hours of summer.

My summer was great.
How was yours?
Did you also happen to meet
the love of your life
one strange morning?

Are you also afraid
that our love will diminish
like a raising moon?
From an immense amber sphere
of mystery into a distant, cold
ring of indifference?

Is this why you keep these secrets?
Oh, yes, you were right.
I cannot put your dog on a leash.
He'll hurt me badly if I try.
Is he just like you?

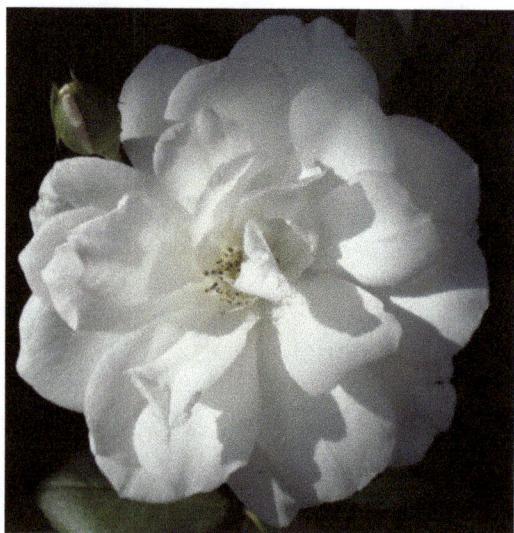

Phone Call Away

When I call you
I hope for the answering machine
I know what to say –
a bit of charm, some irony, laughter

When you answer
I'm at a loss for words
talking too much, revealing things
that should stay secret

When you call
I'm flustered, so surprised
I pretend I don't know you –
it is true, for I don't

Any way you'd look at this
it's absurd – anything you'd say
highlights the nonsense

We are well beyond non-belonging –
We live in parallel universes –
Different streams of time
carry us to contradictory destinations

Still, I cling to a straw of hope
that our day's white passion
could become life's rainbow
if we try

The Bluest

Did you know that your time is blue
like my eyes? Your watch says so
ticking off the hours without me

Did you know that the time for us
is here now? Each minute – a grain
on the sandy beach of denial
measured by heartbeat

I do I do I do

I wonder when you will notice
the pattern painted for us
on black threads you had tarnished

The Weaver made it with brightness
of shy love in the spring that sparkles
at dawn with birdsong

Crystallization

No Juliette, no Ophelia,
I can live without you
while you live on within me

your roots deep
in the core of my being –

in the heart of dark matter
that exploded into
a supernova of our love

I remember the lotus
smoothness of your muscles
caressing my skin –

hot taste of your lips
that worshiped the goddess –

surprise that softened your eyes
when you danced inside
led on and on by my song

Love crystallized
in the density of air
measuring the space

between us

Magic

You are a true magician:
In one day, you changed my death wish
into the gift of breathing deeply
looking with delight on arid desert
from whence you came.

Overwhelmed with gratitude
I walk with a secret smile, dazzling
passers-by, bewildering my neighbors.

Each night, each morning, I read
two books: The Book of Great Love
telling me I'm safe in God, leading me
into freedom, mystic joy
and the little book of our love
that I write, day by day, as I see you.

Three minutes in three days –
what a gift you made
of your presence.

I know: we do not belong
together in ordinary world.

Yet, we are one in God's grace
not to mention the affection of our dogs!

You wrap me in a cloud of peace
measured by your heartbeat –
the one man who could ever
be my Beloved.

Prayer of the Unseen

Thank you, God, for giving me my body –
this most exquisite instrument of pleasure
and thank you for giving me the man
to share it with

On the day that you come
he will see and his eyes will open

and he will see and his eyes will open

and he will –

        – will open –

              – open –

and he will see as you see

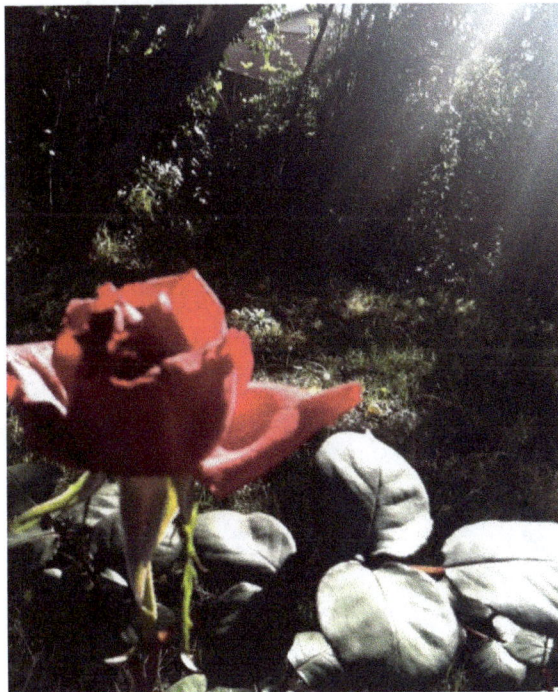

Really

I've never done so much
to destroy a love, yet it lives on,
lingers in the corners of my soul,
explodes like summer fire, joy ineffable

con moto, agitato

I've never seen so much beauty
in one body, outlined by a halo of grace,
smooth lover's sweat at midnight,
bright morning sunrays, light invincible

sotto, colla voce

I've never felt so much
desire, blinding me to all
but your heartbeat, the warm touch
of your strength, dangerous charm

semplicemente

I've never dreamed so much
of a happy future, two strangers
who share nothing, just surprise
at the unthinkable bliss of chance

molto scherzando

I've never loved so much

Indebted

I owe you
twenty thousand
orgasms

by the river
by the tree
at noon
at moonrise
in the air
on the softness
of our pillows

like butterflies
they flew out
of my hands
when you left

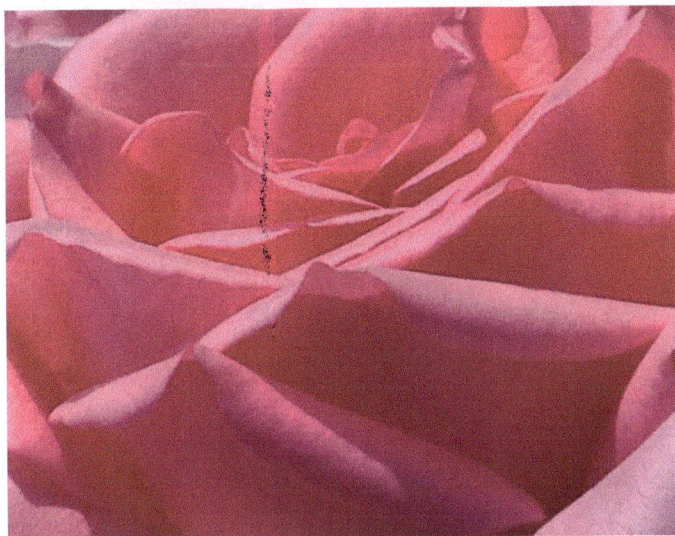

Within

Do you know that my love
is like a puzzle
without an answer?

A rosebush, with opulent
carmine flowers, trusting
in the defense of sharp thorns

It rests among the flutter
of monarch butterflies,
the scent of orange blossoms

Intricate within,
it is a labyrinth with a hundred
entries and no way out

In the aurora of my love,
you see your path for a while,
the path to goodness

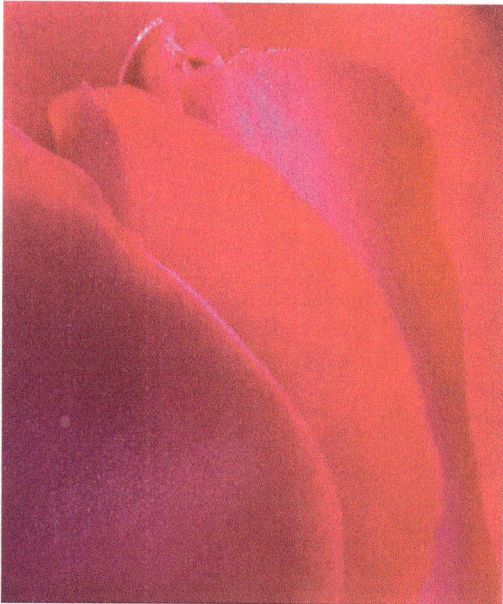

Philadelphia

I found another reason to love you
in Carpenters' Hall, Philadelphia.

The beginning
of their great adventure
and of mine – this was the proof
of the validity of it all,
the confirmation of purpose.

Without power
over you I have nothing,
but the purity of my affection.

It comes by stealth, unwanted
unannounced – it overwhelms
me in the cross-shaped room
once holding the future
of your nation, just as the crossroads
of our chance encounter
held the future of my heart.

I know less and less each day
and I am grateful
for the ancient carpenters
who made your country
and for you, a carpenter
who made me
from the hard wood of sorrow
that softened
under your skillful touch
into love.

Eagle Rock

I drive over the hill
into Eagle Rock,
a messy playground
of your childhood –
an abyss of longing
opens inside me

> (affettuoso)
> I want you all
> I want you now

Wide-eyed boy watching
a pig roasting on spitfire,
angry voices, men fight,
Dad hurling brothers
into the wall

> (con fuoco)
> I want you now
> I'll eat you whole

Tall, lanky teen
roaming wild with buddies,
stealing the first kiss,
the next, and the next –
no girl was free
from dreaming

> (grazioso)
> I want your fingers
> to play a game of rainfall
> on my skin

I keep driving,
searching for the street
I can't remember
Hazelwood? Rockdale?
Somewhere between
Oxy and York?

(con amore)
I want the hurt man
carved from absence
by desert winds and sun

I look for that moment,
suspended in mid-air,
when, trembling,
I took your face in my hands,
kissed you and found
Eagle Rock's greatest gift

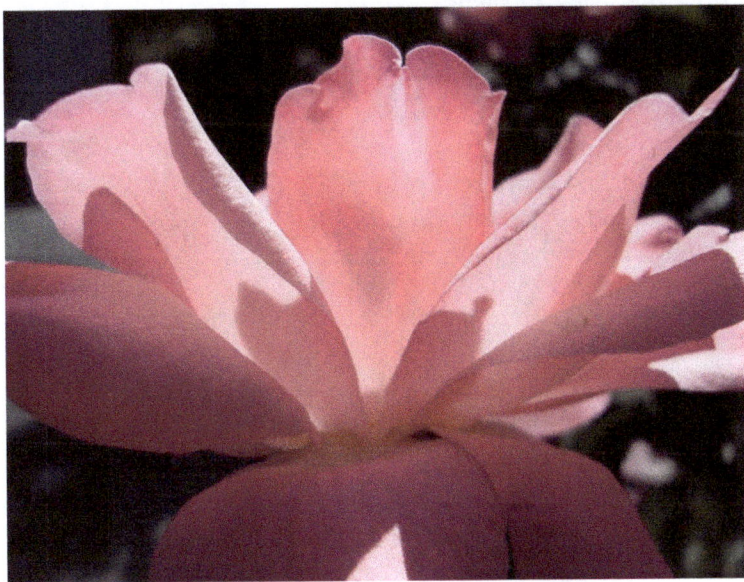

Closeness

I lift my face to the sun
when you walk by
on Tuesday morning.

The searing whiteness
burns away all impurities,
blazes into pure being, peace.

In line to the elevator
I sense you standing close by,
wrapped in my scent with vanilla
and White Diamonds, almost
touching the small of my back.
That's why I take off my sunglasses
as we step in and pick our floors.

You look straight into my eyes.
Flame passes between us.
Time stops, in silence.

    *

*   *

You asked for it, remember?
You said – "I want you now."
You have what you want.

Clarity

I trim my love
to manageable proportions

It grows back
threatening the tidy garden
of my life

I had emptied it
of unneeded passions,
filled with books and roses

again, here you are,
returning
I don't see for what

there's nothing here for you

nothing –
unless you simply come to give

Planting

The garden
is getting out of hand
I have too many trees –

the one
in the blue pot –
a jacaranda
is not doing well

sharing
tight space
with some wild sapling

that grew
from a seed
brought by birds

I will ask my neighbor
to plant it at a street corner

I will not say it is that corner

I will not share my secret

Blessings

First, I loved a man,
then, a dog he brought –
so faithful, like no other –
he adored me. Then,
I loved a tree.

Two trees, rather, intertwined
from roots to branches –
the fragile beauty with bluest flowers
among gently trembling lace of leaves
dancing in the wind – so exotic! –
and a strong, native one
that grew single-mindedly,
against all odds, one hot summer.

A velvet ash, *Fraxinus velutina*,
it announces a fiery end
to fleeting spell of the senses.

They move in a startling image
of lightning that struck the lawn
where I saw a man, his dog, and his love.

What about the Keeper of the tree?
The one who cares for this marvel?

He drove off in his truck to fix
another broken house, heart, whatever.

That's the love I don't want to forget
when counting my blessings.

A Dirge

I'm singing a dirge for the tree,
for the one that died too young –
when the leaves turned dark and brittle
and dry twigs snapped in my fingers
like fuel for winter's fire

I'm singing a dirge for my hope
that shone like the green of cat's eyes
but withered, misplaced in the hours
of longing – it vanished, stifled by lies

I'm singing an ode to the sky,
wisdom of stars in their orbits,
galaxies' laugh at the antics
of constellations running to hide
in infinite heart of dark matter,
from the blaze of last, loving *fiat* –

let it be – let it be light – let it be now –

Radiant

My love is a cloud of peace
settling on stormy waters
of my torn feelings

covering past wounds
with a gentle bandage
of non-remembrance

My love is a healing potion,
a laugh elixir,
an alembic of delight

It fills my days with radiant
color, it scatters gems
on plains of sadness

My love is a mystery to me
no wonder, you also
can't believe it

It's Wonderful

So wonderful.
I'm bewildered by the magic
of life where you are
a part of me
forever.

I've studied hard:
your eyes, sharp contours
of your cheeks, I've learnt them.
Now I know. I see you
when I want to.

I'm so well-versed
in imaginary love,
soon, I won't need
what's real.

Night Trees

Days come and go,
the earth keeps turning,
I stay still.

You drive down my street,
come back for another look.
What do you want to see?

Love is not an easy thing
to manufacture.
I make it in large dollops,
served like ice cream
in cups of kindness.

I package it
in *dulcet* tones
of good memories.
It is expensive,
also, quite refined.

It is perfect that way.
The world is, too.

Oceans breathe.
Stars do not ask questions.
Night trees sleep
with birds in their branches.
Purple mountains
grow more distant,
settling into calm.

By Chance

In s grocery store,
I stop by the bakery,
wondering what to buy.
A tired man turns to look at me.
Maybe because my hair is wet
from my afternoon swim?
Or is it that black dress
with blue flowers?
I wore it when we
first went out, long ago.

I smile when I recognize
your eyes. Such intense,
brown sweetness, such charm.

I turn and walk away.
You leave.

What else is there
to be said?

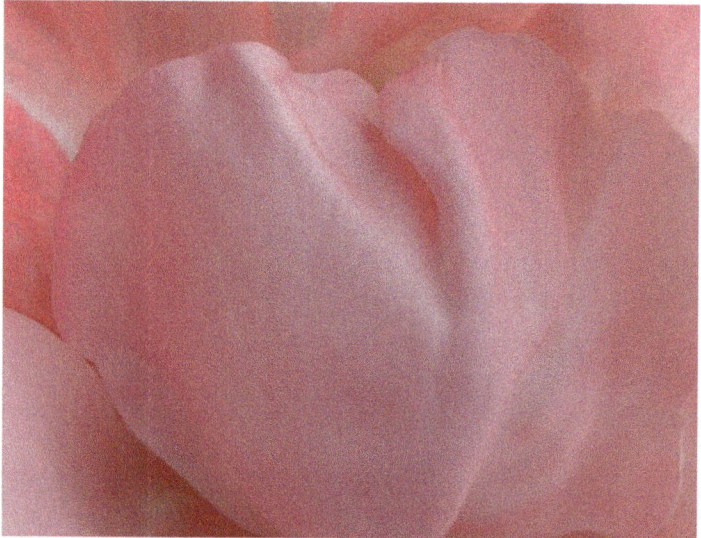

"Look at me..."

- inspired by Ella Fitzgerald's "Misty" and
a Sunday drive to a Buddhist peach orchard

the dark honey of Ella's voice
filled the valley with a golden sheen

The bike stopped at the red light.
The biker looked at me intently.
All in black leather, he did not seem familiar.

the dark honey of Ella's voice
spilled onto the asphalt

The light changed to green. I was touched
by the brightness in his eyes as he drove by,
turning his head, clearly off-balance. He stopped
to gaze at my metallic Honda. I felt his surprise.

the dark honey of Ella's voice
blossomed in an aftertaste of sweetness

I knew he realized who I was,
the woman he found irresistible again
and again and again. I wonder if he told
his girlfriend about our sunny encounter.

the dark honey of Ella's voice
flowed over the wonderland —
the dark honey, oh, the dark honey

The country road led me towards live oak
and grassy slopes, shining yellow and bronze.
There was no hatred, just being alive
after the storm. I was silent. I had nothing to say.

Hope

One day, this love will go away of its own,
it will fade like an overripe rose in the summer,
disappear like Fellini's ancient frescoes.

Not right now, today it is still new,
its luscious blossoms flourish in sunlight.
The delicate, fragrant petals open to sing
under Piero della Francesca's turquoise sky.

One day, the feeling will wane
by itself with the setting moon,
cold, enormous, mysteriously brilliant.
Its light changes the world into a fairy-tale –

"Once upon a time
there was a sleeping beauty
and a carpenter kissed her.
She awoke into a new life
of his presence."

One day, perhaps –

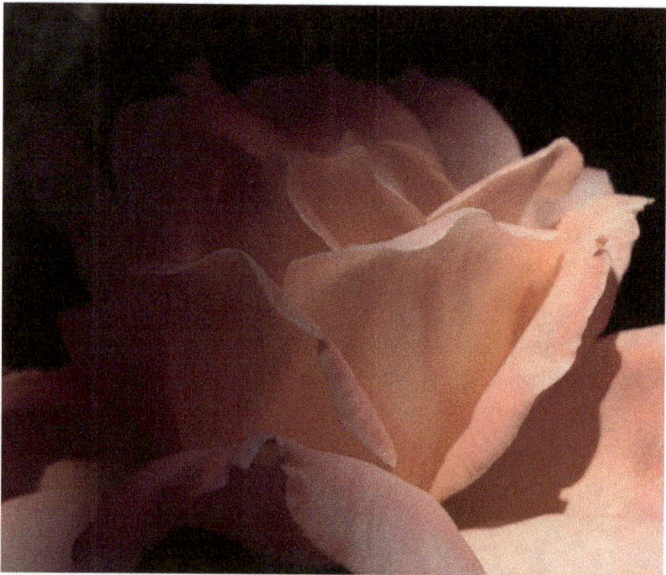

Tiger Nights

Someone nailed gold-plated clouds
to the hard, polished turquoise of the sky.

Striated, like the stripes of a tiger
I did not know I had for a pet

until he bared his teeth
at the dogs flowing through the air

to corner him in my backyard.
The blond fur glistened in shadows.

Three golden labs growled
at the cat the size of a calf.

He turned. His stripes shone
with danger. I woke up afraid.

Now I watch the gold of the clouds
change into orange, scarlet and amaranth

in a quickly darkening cupola
that rests on the hills

above the Hollywood Bowl.
Smooth tones of Joshua Bell's violin

glow in the air, escaping
the relentless chase of the brass.

Wind snatches notes from the bow,
plays with their glossy sheen.

Stars blossom on cloud-stems
in bouquets, wild as tiger lilies

you gave me that night.
Danger lurks in your smile

as you caress my ear
with a whisper: "Remember?"

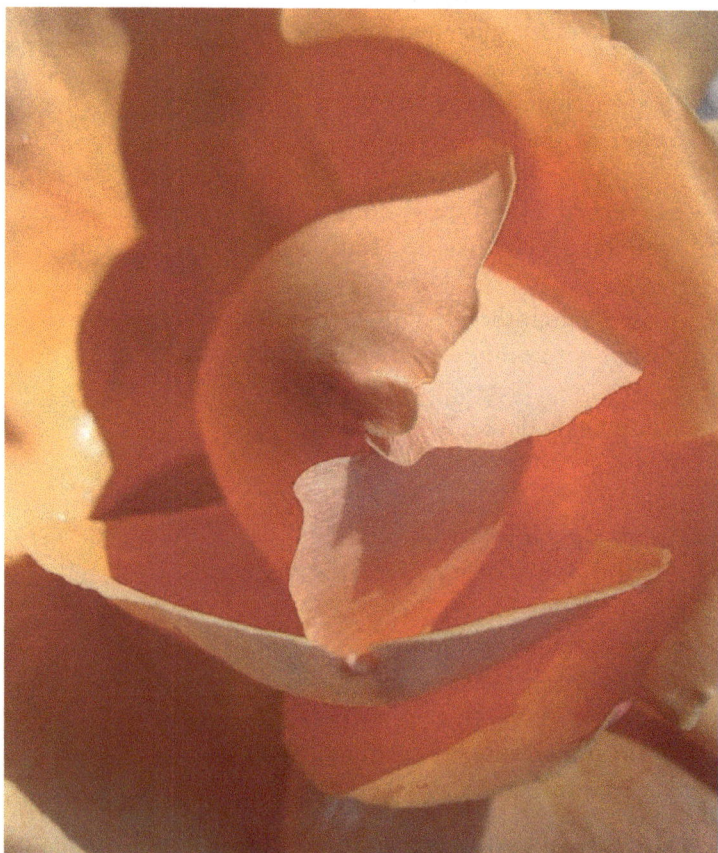

The Music Box

What the world needs now
is love, sweet love…

My china music box plays a song
from your childhood.
Under the lid with one pink rose
I keep my sentimental treasures –

The miniature portrait
in a grey enamel frame echoing
the color of your tank top,
worn in defiance
of my sophistication.

The white tulle ribbon – a memento
from my wedding gown?
It held the ornament up
on the bough of the Christmas tree
after that second, numinous summer.

My broken ring, bent not to be worn again,
 with a deep scar from your blunt saw,
a shape marked by the strength of your fingers.

The missing ring piece hit the ceiling
when it broke off with the pent-up energy
of unwanted love – the marriage that wasn't.

It is somewhere in the corner
of the coldest room in my house.

This was a moment of liberation –
I don't have to – anything – any more.

The three little diamonds –
faith, hope and love – embedded
in the scratched gold, still shine,
though not as brightly as the forty-three
specks of light surrounding your face.

What else? Three dry leaves
from the ash tree that grew by itself,
at the corner where we met. It died,
unwelcome. The Cross of Malta,
waiting to shine on your chest.

*   *   *

*What the world needs now
is light, God's light. . .*

My music box plays on. I make up the words
just as I made up this love of clay and gold,
the dust of the earth and starlight –
partly fragile and partly eternal.

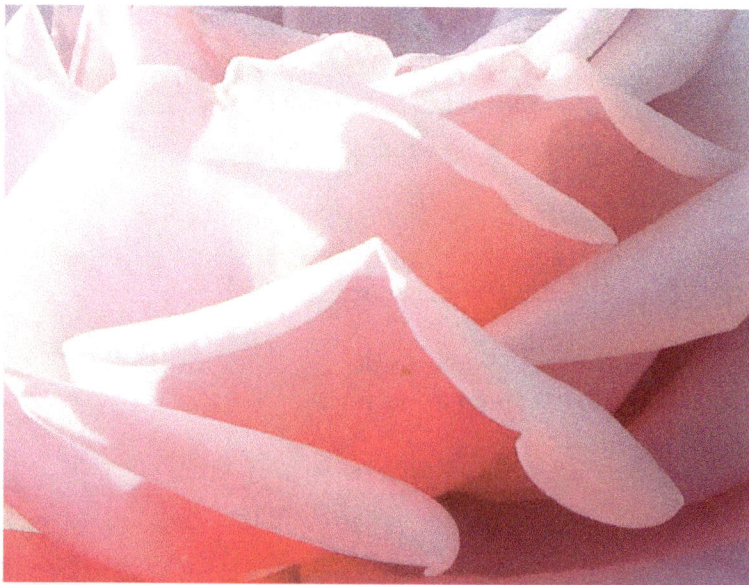

Painting

Olive, sky blue
milk chocolate

dark-red smoothness
bronze, indigo

delicately pinkish
bright white and gold

shine in a serenity rainbow
painted over the blackness

of time by broad, swift
brushstrokes of Mercy

Ultraviolet

Very interesting – these shades of feeling

First, golden blaze of setting sun,
streams of yellow light
blinding me on the freeway
like your closeness blinded me
to your faults, so I came even closer –

Second, the glistening smoothness
of your athletic body, shining
like a Greek youth on an ancient vase,
Orion of the stars in indigo night –

Third, black hue of exhaustion
permeating my whole being,
an affliction settling in my blue eyes –

or does it? I'm not sure about it,
or about anything at all
in the purple haze of my life

forever changed by the unnamable
shared revelation of loving,
you and me in the infinity of grace –

ultraviolet, the end of the rainbow

Revelation

The more I love
the more dangerous
life becomes
in its graphic beauty –

carved with a dagger
stolen from time –

The blade cuts
old wounds open –

It slides on the skin
of the moment –

pierced by knowing –

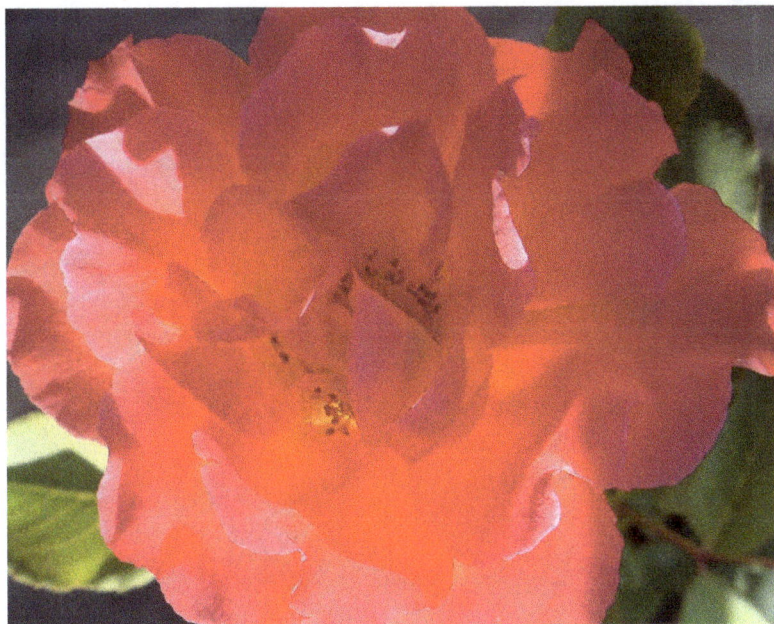

Song of Gratitude

Filled with gratitude, I'm sleepy,
ready to purr with contentment
like a midnight cat.

A smile plays in the corner
of my mouth, full of your kisses –
the softest, gentlest kind.

My lungs expand with fresh evening breeze
bearing a hint of orange blossoms.
Too early for jasmine.

My eyelids close. I live in the moment
of togetherness. I listen
to the monotone chant of a mourning dove.

I watch the ruckus of house sparrows.
Oblivious to a blue jay's shadow,
they fight for breadcrumbs I scatter

on a cement path overgrown with weeds.
Grass sprouts through the crevices.
Life is stronger than stone.

I'm grateful for each breath
filled with loving you. I know,
in being yours, I tasted perfection.

The Good One, the All-Knowing
Wisdom will not deny my prayers.
Shameless, insistent, I'm the dove

that refuses to be silent. This is my song.
This is my litany, my amen:
"Let it be, God, let him be."

KNOWING

DILECTIO

Turquoise and Gold

Of all the loves in the world
yours is the purest –
of all the smiles
yours is the most endearing

You know my secrets,
you care if I cry –
we met to share
the bliss of looking
at the turquoise sky

that never was so blue
before or after –
with gold clouds
scattered like kisses
on time's soft veil

My Quest

Your fingers touch my cheek,
your lips brush against mine.
This explosion wakes us up. We both wake
from the winter of cold machinations:

"If I' do that she'll give me…"
"If I say that, he'll change…"

We dance to the syncopated drums
of our hearts, straining
when our breaths accelerate
and the lighting parts the clouds
of unknowing and ancient wisdom
shines upon the valley.

I've worn out three pairs of iron
shoes, an iron staff, searching for you.
I gave you the coat I made –
a silky, silly coat of affection
to wrap you in the waltz of high sky.

I found you – as the Gypsies say –
in the golden holiness of a night
that will never be seen again
and will never return.

Thanksgiving

I'm grateful for your beauty
I won the lottery when I met you

You lifted the cloud off my days
you filled me with giggles –
how silly can a grown man be?

Rainbows color my clothes –

deep red for love, blue
for innocence, and light brown
for the caramel of your eyes

At church, I join the procession
to the altar, bearing the gift
of faith in fairy-tales

Sometimes you have to
cross the world twice over
to find your true love

A Portrait in Brackets
(Eidetic Reduction)

I love every hair on your head,
every wrinkle, the round scar
in the middle of your forehead
like Cain's mark – you are
the chosen one, the untouchable.

The little freckles on your nose
shine – endearing, childlike.
It was supposed to be
summertime when they came.
Here's summer all the time, already.

My love stirs for your full, half-open lips
waiting for my kisses, as I caress
the sharp contours of your cheeks –
I hold them in my cupped hands
looking straight into your eyes.

There is no world,
only us and the birdsong
at noon in my garden.

I love the quiet confidence
of your fingers, skillful hands
like my father's – solid, able
to fix things, take care of me.

I touch your skin, tracing a line
from your forehead, down the nose,
soft lips, and chin. I brush against
the prickles of your goatee, before
reaching a sweet spot on your neck.

Below your shoulders, under
the smoothness of hard muscles,
the bell of your heart welcomes me.
The blood sings in your veins, love
surges towards me – *I do I do I do*

I rest my head on your chest
and listen to your heart
that beats and beats and never
stops playing the music.

The Other Shore

I'm falling into you
I'm drifting to love's distant shore

to rest with you on your pillow
to whisper my sweet secrets

while you hold me tight
for eternity keeping me from grief

From sorrow into bliss we awaken –
after a long, arduous journey

We've seen marvels on the way
treasures hidden during years

marred by sorrow – now revealed
by luminous brightness that we found

From our New World
we came back changed –

Calmer, wiser, more delighted
with the very act of Being:

"I am, who I am."

Garden of Delight

For you, I'm a pear
with persimmon flavor
bathed in vanilla milk,
my skin is smooth, electric,
it tingles when you touch me

I sing –

Of all the gardens of the world
all the orchards
all the fruit-bearing trees
all the roses

I'm the richest
my blossoms – most abundant
my fragrance – the rarest
beyond reach

Beyond Dark

I just wanted to look
into the white flame
of Love-Ever-Now
in your knowing eyes

You said –
"I'll look, if I want to"
"Don't look, then"
I answered

We went up in a blaze
of wildfire

burning –
burning –

stronger –
deeper –

united –

in love –
in desire –

You touched me
I got my glimpse
of your beauty
to keep me safe
in the darkest hour

Flying

If I had wings
I would fly into your arms
right this second

I would fly like a dove
to find peace

lightly

smoothly

I would come

oh, yes

I would come

Forever

You are my now and forever
to the end of time
spilling charm after charm
over me

You are in me –

for infinity
of feeling

in me –

for a new
beginning

in me –

tenderly

in me –

in me –

in me –

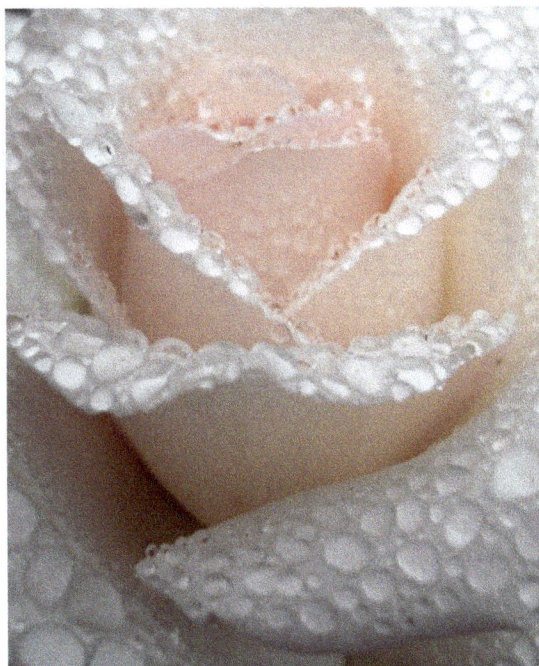

Liquid Grace

I am swimming –
the smooth blue surface
breaks into twin golden ripples
under the rhythmic motion of my body

I am swimming –
each measured gesture
takes me closer to the edge
of the pol – one two one two one two

I am swimming –
you wait, arms open
to welcome me in a sanctuary
of bronze strength, droplets of water

I am swimming –
caressed by the flow,
with eyes closed, head tilted
in sunlight, you wait for my kiss

I am swimming –
to rest my head on
your shoulder in that sweet spot
where life is not dangerous, I'm home

Ella's Voice

I'm constantly dizzy
I don't walk, I dance
All I see is you —
everywhere

My Alpha and Omega
my end and my beginning

Your gestures on constant replay
You walk toward me
again and again
closer

I sing with the Great Ella
"I – is – your woman – now"

True

I'm proud of you, my love
I taught you to speak
without burning God's ears
with curses – I'm grateful

for the kindness in your eyes,
for your look of a streetwise urchin
laughing at his puzzled lady –

I know you, I know who you are,
I don't know what

The most astoundingly
handsome, seductive,
masculine and loving man
I ever knew?

I never knew?

Crescent of Wonder

Frogs' screeching chorus
welcomes me in the evening.
Crescent moon smiles
like a Cheshire Cat

No Alice, I am in a Wonderland
of cabbage-size rose blossoms
and four-inch dragonflies
in phosphorescent orange

hovering above desert stream –
rocks covered with green algae
under the bluest intensity of indigo sky

At night, when the flood of rain
pounds on my roof, I wonder
about the man of this land,
the perfect man

whose existence I still question,
doubting the testimony of lunar insight.
Yes, the moon saw us together –
that's why it still smiles

Snowfall

My love is like the weather –
good or bad, it simply is

and you have to live
with the heat of passion,
with the cold of indifference,
with the rain of tears
spilled over lost chances,
dreams, hopes – broken

you have to live
with the snow of gentle kisses
falling all over your body,
covering you with a soft blanket
of innocence and peace

A Snow Valentine

Snowflakes fall
outside my window
Hypnotized, I fall
dancing with them –

I love you now.
I loved you yesterday.
I will love you tomorrow.
It feels good to be timeless –

Permanent
fixed in a beauty
that does not crack or fade
like red rocks eroding into sand –

The intensity
of living in the present
is bewildering – life sparkles,
like crystalline spring of fresh water –

Still as a meadow
silenced by the softness
of snowflakes, I love you now –

No longer tired,
I rest in the warm glow
of the afternoon's diffuse light –
it whitens all snow-covered branches –

My heart beats with
the rhythm of affection
for the unseen –

Plato was right –
He died two thousand years ago
and still he is right –

Beauty and goodness
and truth are three perfect
facets of a divine crystal –

lost in an empty universe –
concealed by flurry of snowflakes –
transformed into love –

Da Capo

You gave me the greatest gift

(immer langsam)

You gave me back my soul
stolen by grief
and treachery of a selfish man,
my life – a toy in his hands,
shattered to please him

(sehr klagend)

You gave me back my body
broken by pain, rejection
of the cruel one – unconcerned,
but for the scheming
of his wicked mind

(noch lieblich)

You gave me back my body,
soul, heart, affection
and a silent glow of serenity
in my eyes

You gave me the greatest gift

The Pearl

When I think of love
I'm so filled with you
I can't put my delight
into words, it is
beyond measure

My eyes change
from anxious into blue
felicity – I'm peaceful,
I found my place on earth

Funny, how chance
drenched me with happiness
after years of woe –
I do not understand
what happened, why?

Will I ever grasp
what it means to be you?
Carefree, under the hot sun?
Not really, but I can tell you
I'll cherish your life forever

A Letter

I cannot believe my luck. Finally,
after all this time, half a lifetime
spent on searching for you.

Here you are, here is your promise.
You write:

And when I lay my head down
at night, I think of you
And when I wake up
in the morning, I think of you
and I'm content
My smile is from ear to ear
I'm so happy
I do not know
what you see in me
I did not know
that such love
even existed

I keep some letters
by my bed, to read
at night for good dreams
and happy waking

Will my nightmares
ever disappear?

Star Gazing

You touched me
so deeply inside
that a new star was born
from my orgasm

subito, sforzando, con brio

Somewhere in the galaxy
the patterns of electrons shifted
in the magnetic current
of desire reaching its climax,
peace of togetherness, awe

tenuto, più mosso rubato

My Alpha and Omega
my end and my beginning

accelerando, allargando
da capo

Arrival

The golden taste of mango
carries the remembrance
of exotic splendor –
your body touching mine
all over

Caressed by sunlight
I revel in the luxury of being
at its most intense –
being one with you

You are the missing piece
in my puzzle –
neither round, nor square,
you fit exactly
in the empty place
by my heart

I can rest now,
my journey's over

I smile
when I look at the sky

I blush
when nobody sees me

I found you –
the perfect man
for my life

Going Home

It feels good
to go back
home to your love
I wear it
as a second skin,
comfortable
like old pajamas

But it is not old –
exhilarating, it grows
ever younger,
still more surprising

All I had to do
was to admit it

Stop trying
to hide it
from myself
in the dark attic
among chimeras
and occult creatures
that could not be

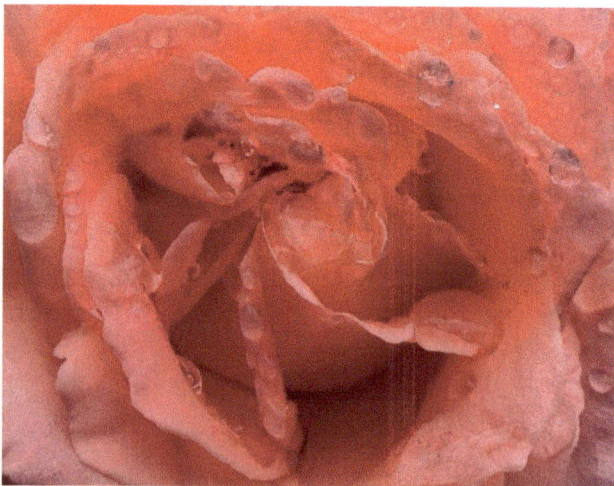

Fairy-Tale Queen

I love fairy-tales
and ancient books of wisdom.
Alone in my garden,
I turn brittle, yellowed pages.
The wind whispers,
stirring the leaves.

...and the Queen, all dressed in gold
walked in, to meet her King.

Delighted by brilliance of her jewels,
the sparkle in her eyes, he trembled.
His heart filled with desire,
he never knew existed. He said:
"You loved me first, I loved you back,
I could not help it." But he lied,
it was at his explicit invitation,
repeated twice, that she came.
Yes, that's what she wanted
most of all since she saw him —
to be his. In light of his perfect beauty,
it was obvious. Her body flourished
under his gaze, a fresh rose
with dew on velvet petals, softer
than silk, more luminous than diamonds.

As she came to her King, the Queen sighed
and smiled to herself one last time,
before finding a new life in his embrace...

Crowning

You are my King of Roses
I taught myself to love you

You are perfect,
because you have so little
I have to love you
for yourself

You said – "I want you now"
Nobody wanted me
like that before

You wondered how you felt me
move and dance with you

I dance for you alone,
no one else

With you, I came back
from Death Valley

To walk barefoot on the grass,
taste the salty warmth
of your skin, look
at your hands

and love them,
kiss you and crown you
my King

Good, Very Good

And God said, "I'll comfort you
like a mother soothing a newborn –
you will rest in my arms, rest in me"

And I dreamt of my day of rest,
the day of our love on the bed of roses

The flickering light of vanilla candles
cast strange shadows on the ceiling
above your smooth, glistening body

And God said, "let us make
man and woman in our image"

And the Day of New Creation
was good, very good, so good –

Remember

You are
the wisdom
of infinite possibility

Each day –
an adventure

Each Saturday –
a game with children
in the park

Each night –
a mystery not to be shared
with strangers

Each kiss –
I'd tell you
but you know

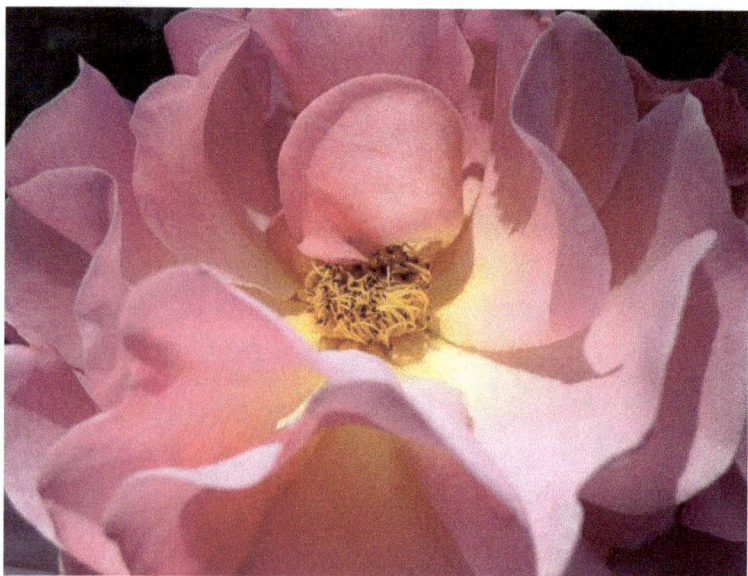

Rose Always

now

The petals
have fallen
and blown away
in a gust of time

It is like a wind-tunnel in here

Change
moving – moving
onward
never stops – never sleeps
onward

I try to keep my rose intact
just one little rose
just one set of petals arranged
in a pink-white harmony
perfectly – just so

In the still point
of the turning wheel
that grinds all –
grinds me into dust
falling between
fingers of Mercy

I'll keep this one rose
this lush, sunny day
brilliance with purplish overtones
gold clouds in blue sky

It will be there
when the spool of my mind
unwinds into infinity

I'll keep my rose
ever lovely
ever new

rose always

just so

now

FEELING

CONSOLATIO

Being

In your absence –

The sky blushes
like a peach at sunset

The rocks grow stronger
satiated with the power
of the earth core

Water laughs in the river
flowing to its end
inexorably

My eyes sparkle
at the thought of you

The world is –
In your absence

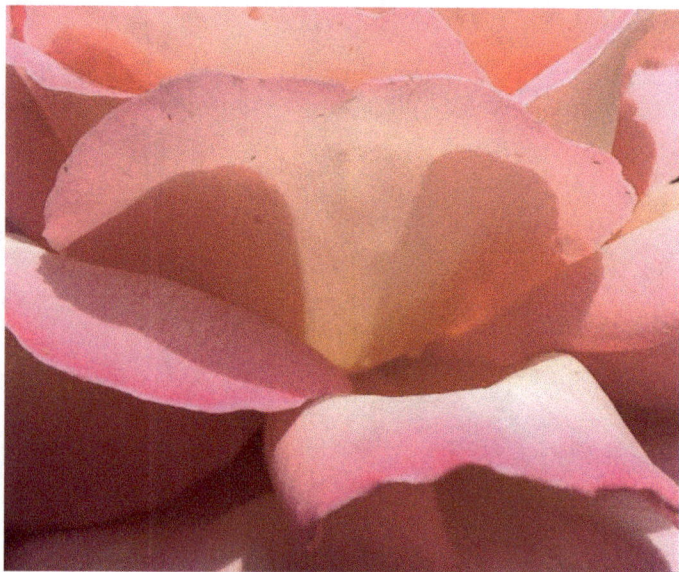

Hurting

Pain is a rose
that grows in the desert,
a rose of mercy

Its white blossoms open
to reveal a secret —

fragrant gold stamens
in a crown of thorns

I can't write an ode
to cuts and scratches

I can't praise the wounds
except the pierced heart of One

called to pass into life
through the curtain of pain

We are alive
if it hurts — we are alive

My rose grows stronger —
crimson blossoms flourish

bringing me back
from the land of illusion

into presence unveiled
by the sharp sting
of pain

Awe

I reached Kierkegaard's point
of Either/Or again – that's where it started

Beyond choices, beneath daily worries,
I saw a strange, omniscient, vivid presence,
the silent One, above all words and limitations,
the Absolute – you'd call it – the Divine

The Dangerous, Infinite, Menacing
if you are sick with ill delight –

The All-embracing, Healing and Sublime
for those who know the Sweetest,
Kindest, most supremely Glorious,
Beautiful, Life-giving God,
the All, the One

Please, God, would you give me
back my true beloved, if I so adore you?
Please, please, please, pretty please?

Silence – Awe

Day by Day

Pink petals cover the grass
when I trim faded roses
falling one by one – drop, drop, drop –
silently, as years fall off my calendar
day by day, day by day,
until nothing remains.

This emptiness glows with peace –
Elation, even. My spirit soars to the sky
with birds – a skylark trills up high
for the sun and meadows,
filled with dew's diamond droplets,
fated to disappear by noon.

The skylark, the morning dew –
that was there and then,
in fields by my grandma's house.

Now a mockingbird's fluted voice
tells me of time passing in my garden.
Drip, drip, drip – like water leaking
from a faulty faucet, years drip away
from my life. I'm weaker, wiser, slightly
more amused with myself. What strange
ideas can a person have? What love?

Barely opened in newness of their buds,
hoping to blossom as summer's queens,
roses shrivel into dear old, crinkly ladies.
Their petals fall – forgotten, useless –
my days fall with them.

Troubles

The mockingbird wakes me up
at five a.m. It sounds like my alarm.

*   *   *

My rose bush died – the one
I planted when we met.
In a week, all leaves dried and fell,
without changing color.

I pulled out the dead plant
and saw an enormous worm,
the ugliest, most hideous thing,
still gnawing at its roots.

*   *   *

Rats moved into my house.
One climbed to the top
of my Christmas tree.

Beady eyes looked at me insolently –
from among green branches.
I put peanut butter in the traps.

Most Wanted

You have sadness of the damned in your eyes
The left, emptied of heartsease –
The right, clouded with despair

Thick lines on your cheeks point downward
A snarling rictus of lips, once moistened with kisses
"There is no hope," you think, "none ever"

What did I expect? You said "No" every time
except when denial was healthy – virus
multiplied in your veins, carved
your grief-stricken face

Rejections do this to you, so does contempt –
You said, "Not in a thousand years,
do not even dream" to yourself
and you stopped dreaming –
to die slowly

In a refusal to breathe in
the light, drink wisdom
from the goblet of fire –

studded with diamonds
of kindness, luminous
outpouring of grace –

Damage Report

There is something in my garden
that eats rosebuds.
It strikes from shadows – each open blossom
a survivor, victorious over the unseen.

Darkness creeps into my rose paradise
of birdsong – it silences
melodious voices of mockingbirds,
busy chatter of sparrows.

I raise my head up like a snowdrop
from under frozen whiteness.
I gently trim damaged branches
to heal their open wounds –

An ancient Druid in disguise
I wait for what I know will happen –
while something born of untold darkness
eats rosebuds in my garden.

Ready to Wear

I'm dressing you in roses
so, you don't have to wear
the heavy sweatpants, block letters
across your thigh – PRISONER

Scarlet blossoms are prettier
than the orange jumpsuit
and shackles on the way
to the courthouse

Sheltered by poetry
you will not have to hide
in lies, deceptions,
color your hair black,
become an enigma
in sunglasses

The blanket I wove
will protect you
from spurious rage
unneeded when the locket
of prayer opens
in an offering to the Unseen

You cannot escape
God's presence. Transparent,
opaque, you will blossom
after the light's blade
cuts the bonds that trapped you
in the cycle of unforgiveness

The Great Beyond

What do they know about love?
Its incandescent beauty
setting the world aflame
even in your absence?

What do they know about hope?
The joyous certainty of being
together in a blessed future
that may not happen?

What do they know about faith?
Not more than we do –
faithless creatures
of deception, secrets

    *   *   *

It is beyond belief
how you loved me

beyond hope
that you do

The Waiting

I open the envelope – a letter
with a newspaper clipping
a bouquet of red roses and a story
about mortgage fraud on the back

You rubbed your soap along the edges
I breathe in your scent after shower

Three phone calls while I was away
eight after I sent you that letter
admitting what it meant to me –
that hot July day, under the tiger sky

Press five if you accept this call –
stay on the line – stay on the line

breathing – dreaming – searching – hoping –
are you ready?

A lifeline – A lifeguard – My lifeguard – Stay –

Lush buds open on a dormant branch
the half-forgotten fragrance
the taste of your sweat on my lips
heavy drops falling from above

The aroma of your bronze, spicy
body – your touch on my skin –
a sudden swell of emotion –
irruption of the past into the present

Stay on the line – accept this call
from an inmate at Avenal State Prison

A long-lost love awakens
with a whiff of newsprint ink
mixed with a faint echo
of what once was, could be, will be –

when we meet on God's mountain
and rosebuds open into a scarlet cloud
that makes the fortuneteller blush
as she sees our future in her Tarot cards

"My love" – you say –

thirty second left –
stay on the line –
stay on the line –

Acceptance

Your lies dance
into the sunset –
I love you

Your mask has fallen
I see who you are –
love blossoms

Your gestures
once beautiful
are ugly

You hurt me –
my love shines
brighter still

It envelops me
like a lightning
of grace –

sudden – holy – unexplained

Orion

I see you in star contours, when I look up,
coming home from a late Christmas party –

My Orion, my bright hunter crossing the night skies
with a bow strung for action

Smooth skin shines over broad shoulders,
three-diamond belt adorns the narrow waist
You are a constellation of beauty

But a seraph? A fallen one? They say
he is "Shemhazai" – the angel who fathered giants,
lured by the silky faithlessness
of golden hair, tresses of seduction.

He crucified himself,
hanging upside down in winter sky,
remorseful, still guilty of desire

It fills you to your fingertips
when your hands join together
at the small of my back
and you pull me closer

Swathed in midnight blaze
I'm waiting for the double helix
of our embrace to twirl higher and higher,
into a brilliant, fluted column
of light –

rising to pierce indigo cupola
where the stars of Orion now sleep
immutable and content
in their silence

Waterfall

It snows on Sunday
Our Lady of Grace church is crowded
with warmly dressed people

I am late. I still wear my gloves
when the vision fills my mind
overflowing with light waves

liquid brightness   spilling   over
*   your naked body   limb   after   limb*
*   after limb   washing   every   inch*
of your skin   your   whole   being
*   cleansed   by   the   luminous   flood*
*   blinding   holiness   grace*

Bewildered, I sing Her praises.

At home, alone in my garden
I rest with eyes closed, face turned
up to the sun. I fall asleep
thinking of this vision
caressed by sunlight

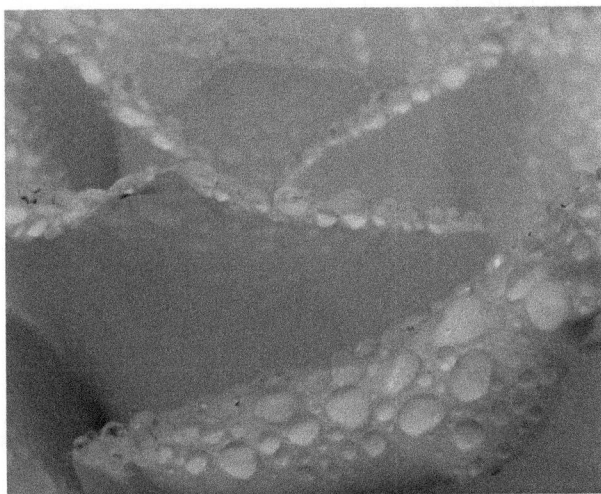

In a Winter Garden

You are responsible, forever, for what you have tamed.
You are responsible for your rose.
~ *Thee Little Prince* by Antoine de Saint-Exupery

When the rose
petals curl inward
in a delicate contour
of the corner of your lips
all that's wrong
with the world fades

Pain dissipates
in the soft pink glow
of the blossoms cut
from antique bushes,
that carry the same gift
for every crying woman

Perfection grows
in the garden. It falls
in a cascade of petals
into the reflecting pool
of happiness – still vivid,
affection – not forgotten

Midnight Fire

*In the golden holiness of a night that will never be seen again
and will never return…* (from a Gypsy tale)

After greeting the New Year with a Chopin polonaise, danced around the hall, down the stairs, out to the patio, I left the laughter of strangers and went home. On the way, I drove down the street of your childhood. It was drenched with the glare of the full moon in a magnificent sparkling halo.

I thought the old house would be empty and dark. I was startled by its brightness. On the front lawn, three boys were jumping around a bonfire. They screamed with joy when the flames shot up to the sky. They called me to join their wild party. The gold reached out to the icy blue light. Sparks scattered among the stars. You were there, hidden in shadows. I sensed your sudden delight.

*my rose diamond brooch
sparkles on the black velvet —
stars at midnight*

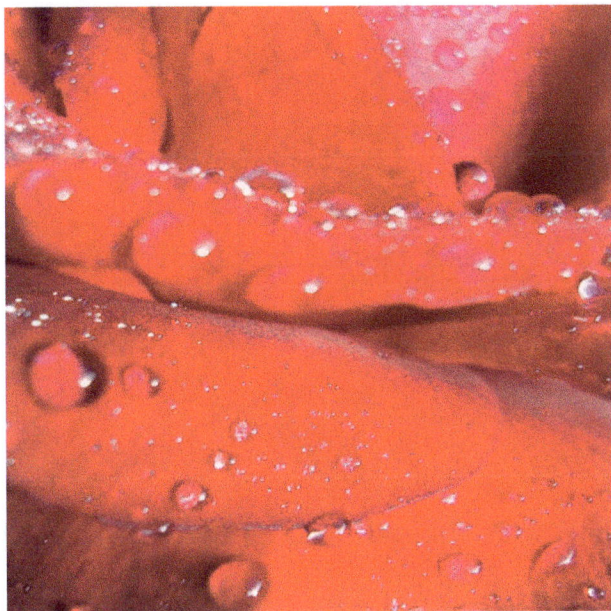

Chaconne in D Minor

This music is for you –
my favorite, a piece of my soul

First – endless grief –
the same pain circles
over and over, round and round –

Then, timeless love –
from peak to peak of passion
tenderness, wistful longing
a kiss and a tear
in the corner of my eye
while the lips are still smiling –

For every lost love
God will give you a new one –

For every tear – a smile –

For every act
of bitter selfishness
a crumb of sweetest grace –

a taste of perfection
in the morning –

Pining

The prickly heat of the summer builds up into a wall of blazing air
hitting me in the face as I open the door to step out onto the patio.
The scent of needles rises from the Japanese pine that grew out of
its tightly trimmed oval shape into a windmill of branches stretching
into the shimmering blue of the sky.

I know you are not coming back. You have been gone for ten years
– long years that sculpted the pine into this chaos of freedom.
A mockingbird on the top twig repeats snippets of birdsong,
whir of hummingbird's wings, the ringing tone of my alarm clock.

> *I dream of your bare skin*
> *glistening with the bronze hue*
> *of dead pine needles*

My Full Moon in September

~ after Clair de lune by Claude Debussy

An orchestra of crickets slices through the night of full moon and shade
piercing my white garden. I look at the contours of clouds
outlined in indigo sky, black pine branches stretching
upwards as the clouds flow faster, faster, faster –
The night twirls around me, the earth
dances with the unseen sun,
circling the galactic core –

Light particles hurl from solar halo, bounce off flat face of the moon
and drop gently onto my retina. Midnight covers my garden
with pixie dust. It glows in the darkness
of our last evening, last summer –

There will never be another night like this –
the full moon smiling in its orange halo, the fat moon
of the blood moon tetrad – ominous and seductive
in its luminescent self. *Shine – yes, shine with me –*
it sings and pleads with its thinly strung voice,
resonating on grass stems, pine branches.

I remember the shape of your head impressed on my pillow
and go inside to snuggle under blankets, still warm
from my sleepy touch.

      Alone in an empty bed,
                I smile –

                wrapped in moonlight
                and the silvery sheen
                of the crickets

Foxes

You called wild desert foxes
to feed them – they ate from your hand
gingerly picking morsels from your fingertips

You tamed barking dogs –
they came to lie down at your feet
happy to obey, quiet, tails wagging

You whispered secrets
in my ears, words of honeydew
and magic – I loved their resonant charm

Then, you lost your voice –
shrouded in suffocating fog
of meth and booze, yes, you lost it

I hear silence now –
see the chaos of vicious
charcoal foxes, with steel-sharp teeth

I wait for a new
dawn – sweet melody
of togetherness to resound again

... Around the Roses

My ring for you is made of light
circling around your finger

My ring for you is too thick,
too uncomfortable to ever be taken
for granted, to ever slip off beyond
the sphere of your awareness

With this ring, you'll think of me
at every sunset, every dawn

My love is in this ring, you know,
the ring you do not want
and are afraid of –

Let me say it again – my ring for you
is made of milky white agate,
a semi-precious, semi-opaque stone
that glows with an internal light
in the noon brightness of the land
of milk and honey –

My ring for you is meant to rest
on your right hand, the open palm
of endless promise –

I also bought a ring for me
thinking I might forget you, after
you'll leave on that long journey
away from me, slowly walking
step by step out of love –

Not Aspartame

You are my daily dose
of sugar – refined from tall cane
that gently bends in life's winds –
reaching for the sun
drinking the soft rain
of my love –

Startled by the whir
of the hummingbird's wings
while it dips its beak
in the scarlet cup of a hibiscus
I sweeten my day with
the thought of you –

I remember the golden glow
of morning light on your skin,
the bright halo surrounding you
on my lawn. In the rainbow
of sprinkler mist I saw
the chosen one, my beloved –

It took generations
to make you – what you are –
you alone know who
you will be when I see you
in my driveway –
again

A Tale of Tomorrow

Once upon a time in a faraway land
there was birdsong in the garden –

shocked into silence by the sudden strike
of a red-tailed hawk that fell like lightning

from wide open sky to grab
a hapless sparrow in its claws

I survived your lightning presence
in my life – shock after shock of discovery

nightly earthquakes of passion
rollercoaster rides from ecstasy to despair

I step carefully now, slowly look around
like a phoebe that musters its courage

to venture out, pick up seeds of contentment
build a nest from broken twigs, dried grass stems

    – there is always tomorrow –
    – remember, always, tomorrow –

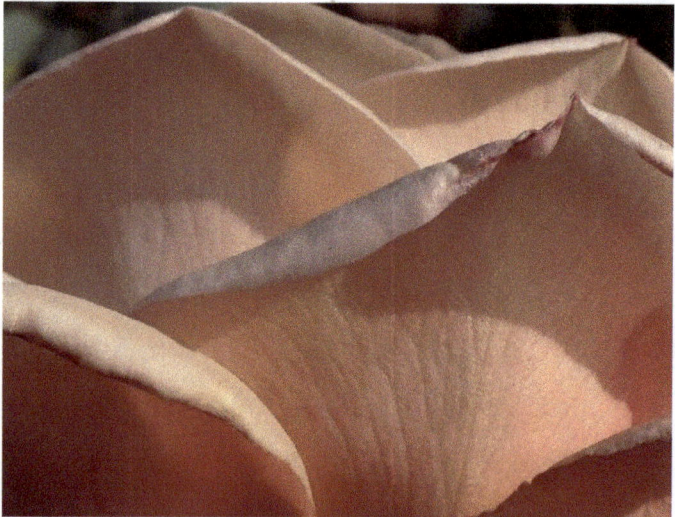

The Way Out

If you feel darkness touching you,
its moving, sticky tendrils reaching out
to wrap around you, its magma
of opaque substance flowing slowly
to envelop and devour you —

Say: *No.*
Say: *Stop.*
Say: *Go away.*

Say:
I'm a sovereign citizen of the galaxy.
I invoke the law of free will.
I refuse to be touched by darkness.
I seek shelter in Divine Light.

Stand firm. Do not fall into the void
of fear, anger, selfish cruelty and hate.

Say:
I ask you kindly, my dark velvet beauty,
leave me, go far away where you belong,
where countless delights await you.
Do not fear Love. Do not fear Light.
Go find your peace. Go find your bliss.

See? The clouds are lifting. Black
cords disappear. Thank Light
for brilliance. Thank Love
for kindness. Thank Life
for the sweetest gifts
only you can find.

What's Possible

There isn't anything
that cannot be forgiven –
know this, my graceful Tiger-Cat

We once held hands
we walked in silence, smiling
under the canopy of ancient oaks

We danced, we talked
I watched the moon's dark circle
eclipse the sun (held safely in your arms)

The past is gone
with shadows, mists at sunrise –
our shared secret will guide us, we'll meet again

I'll wait for you
to join me for a lifetime –
all is well, all shall be well, when we love

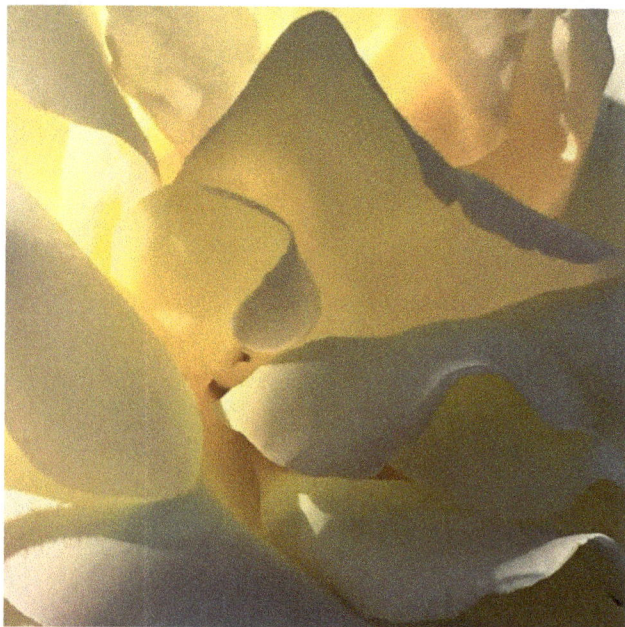

New Beginning

Let's start from the spot of light
by your right eye. You see some goodness
in the world. That speck of white
by your ear? – You hear the truth –
even if it does not stick.

There is, then, brightness
of my broad-rimmed hat
reflected onto your cheek –
but merely, slightly, there is
not enough radiance, I guess

Find more light within –
close your eyes to the passing
form of this world and listen
to pure song that you sing

An ocean waits for you
to traverse its hidden depths

Deep in your heart
the sweetest voice

is calling –

calling –

calling –

A Walk in the Canyon

We walk on layers of
past lives. Fossilized shells
skin, bone, membrane.
Ripples in sand on ocean floor
now frame mountains.
Patterns sculpted by waves
linger on after water disappeared.

Sand, sandstone, limestone.
Granulated, petrified by time.

falling— sinking – twisting – rising up

Like grains of sand caught by cosmic tide
we rise and fall with the shifting clouds
of light and darkness. Words
change us into stone. Words
melt us in the fire of compassion.

Like water, we flow and disappear,
droplets of rain in mountain streams
racing down the slopes, through valleys,
searching for the ocean.

The beating wings of the dove
struggle against the wind.

falling— sinking – twisting – rising up

Tiger Dreams

And so, it happened – at last,
you're here, fast asleep on my lawn
in fated corner where I once
saw a tiger-cat with bared teeth

You look so childish now
curled, a helpless baby
with gold hair shining
in the morning light

Are you a tiger or a cat?
Or a chameleon – shifty,
dangerous, without mercy
in black diamond eyes?

No matter what, my heart's
wide open. You are my choice.
Love conquers all – they say.
I'm good with that.

A Ballad of New Heart

Once I found a rock heart, my heart of hard rock.
I took it to carry with me.

Along muddy shores of the river of time
that flows down in the ravine.

I carry my rock as I walk up the hill
of a thousand stones, all so cold.

The rock now softens and moves in my hands,
it melts into heart of pure gold.

I carry my gold heart up the mountain, up high,
I carry, I carry its weight.

With each step it's heavier, its surface so hard.
Careful! it might slip out of my hands.

I know how the river races down, full of mud.
I'm lucky, I turned to go up.

This weight is for me to carry alone.
It is my heart of rock, my own task.

It starts feeling alive, in the warmth of my hands.
I thought it was only a rock.

I cradle it safely in my two folded arms
as I bring it up high, to the top.

Here the sky is clear blue. Winter storms have all passed.
I look at smooth river below.

I thought it was muddy, full of dirt as it rushed,
but it sparkles with rainbows aglow.

It's my river that flows, my heart changed to flesh.
I discovered my treasure of old.

You will, too, find your heart, change your rock into gold
to cherish, to love, and to hold.

A Ballad of New Sun

You have seen your golden wings
~ Rumi

He came out of nowhere with head bowed down low
in shame and in sorrow, contrite.

His face wrapped in shadows, cloak black as a tombstone,
he came out of nowhere at night.

He stood there before her with head bowed down low
asking silently, asking for love.

Her hands on his chest, his heart beating wildly,
steady current flowed out from her palms.

Light and Love, Light and Love, so much Light, so much Love,
the black cloak broke stiffly in half.

Rays of bright light exploded: he flew out of his cage –
in a lightning, a flash of delight.

He was free, she was thrilled. Two halves of dark shell
fell down on the ground far below.

In brightness most fine with high outstretched arms
he rose up, in the birth of new dawn.

But did he have wings? We don't know, we can't tell.
It looked like, maybe, he did.

Could he fly? He did fly, bursting out of his shell
like a phoenix, a comet, a kid.

In a lightning of love, he ascended so free
shining true — a phoenix of might.

She was happy and glad. She laughed out so loud –
such miracle, the dream of her heart.

There's a new Star, new Sun as he glows, laughs and shines,
turning midnight into high noon.

In a whirlwind of rays, comets, stardust and sparks,
divine brightness, more dazzling than Moon.

He's her brother reborn, gold prince of new dawn,
floating on clear weaves of fire and air.

Her job here is done, two hands on his chest
healing, breaking the spell of despair.

Oh, sweet love to heal him. Oh, sweet love to free him.
The One Love that flows through her arms.

No matter how dark, no matter how lost,
we can wake, we can shine, become stars.

We are free, we can fly, high above midnight sky.
So much Love, so much Light, so much care.

It's for us that this Love flows so brightly tonight,
and we sing of new life, of new world.

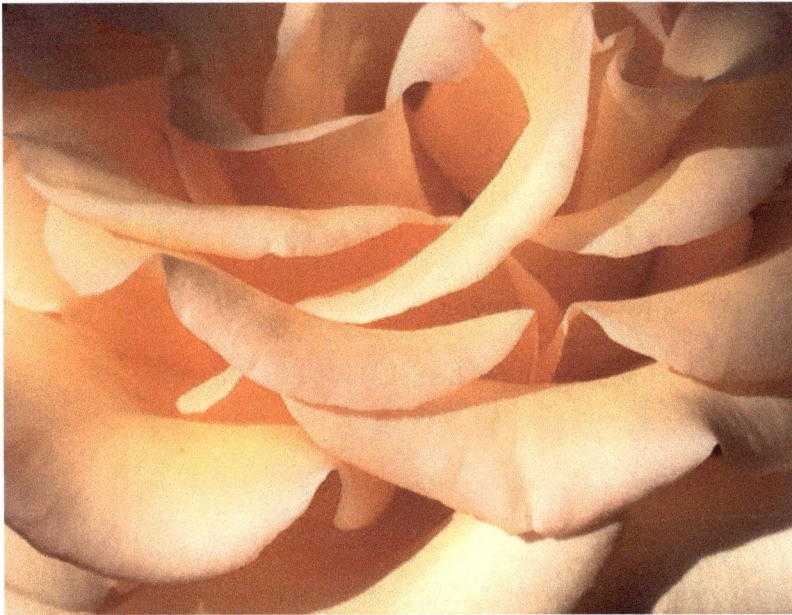

A Ballad of Golden Scroll

Once she saw a path of shadow leading straight to her back,
stretching far, into mists, into void.

With black fog swirling 'round, it was made of despair,
guilt, shame, and remembrance of wrongs.

Now the Sun rose within her, its light poured out through.
She was brighter than bright Morning Star.

It was time to let go, end this lesson of pain.
The Sun's brightness was seen from afar.

She rolled up this path of shades and of mists
'round the black hole of tears and regrets.

As it rolled like a carpet, she saw gold underneath,
cobwebs over brilliant gold nets.

The roll was too heavy for her to take up.
She called "help!" Angels knelt on both sides.

All of Light, all in white, they shone as they knelt
on one knee, with the scroll of her past.

She looked closer, but now only one angel stayed,
shadows wrapped up in dazzling light.

Her past faults and her hurts, he held in both hands.
He was kneeling, her angel at night.

She could see his white wings, opened wide, full of Light,
their long tips stretched far, north and south.

The pathway behind her was clear, pure and gold,
shining brightly and smooth like a pearl.

She tied silver cord around the scroll and said "Fly!"
End to end of horizon, his wings.

With one sweep, he rose up, carrying her heavy load
to release it on currents of wind.

High above was the speck, in the sky, in the Sun.
It exploded in a shower of sparks.

His huge wings filled the air with his delighted song.
With sweet voice, tender song of her heart.

Pain was gone, she was free. It was bright all around.
Light aglow in her body, her veins.

You should know there's a myriad of angels around.
They will help you break your own chains.

My Gifts

...the necklace of songs, that you take as a gift
~ Rabindranath Tagore

I gather sunlight
in my palms
to save for later
when it's dark outside
and hope seems lost.

My hands are full
of brightness.
I gingerly carry
the tangle of sunrays
in a procession of gifts,
down the aisle.

I gather sunlight
to keep close
to my heart,
and warm us
through cold
winter nights
with a rich glow
of sunfire.

How to Cross the Great White

We are almost there. The pink
stretch of light on the horizon.
The luminescent arch above
thick trunks, crowned with the lace
of twigs and branches. A gathering
of trees calls us. Almost.

We have to cross the salty plain
without life — white, bone-quiet,
it stretches into the distance, pulls us
within — to forget, to linger, to remain
lonely, immobile, transfixed. Almost.

We look up to the ribbon of light
above the horizon. It shines
like a crystal egg of rose quartz,
the sign of solace, understanding.
We raise our gaze higher, to the aqua,
pearlescent, indigo firmament,
with trillions of stars – watching,
unblinking.

Each step takes us further, closer,
as we search for the contours
of Orion, his belt lost among
untold treasures.

Scattered nodules of light
sail through space,
sing the morning anthem.

Dawn's first birds stir in branches,
comb their rainbow feathers,
wait for the awakening Sun.

Eons pass. We walk
through the great absence.

Our steps echo
in the vaults of the Night.

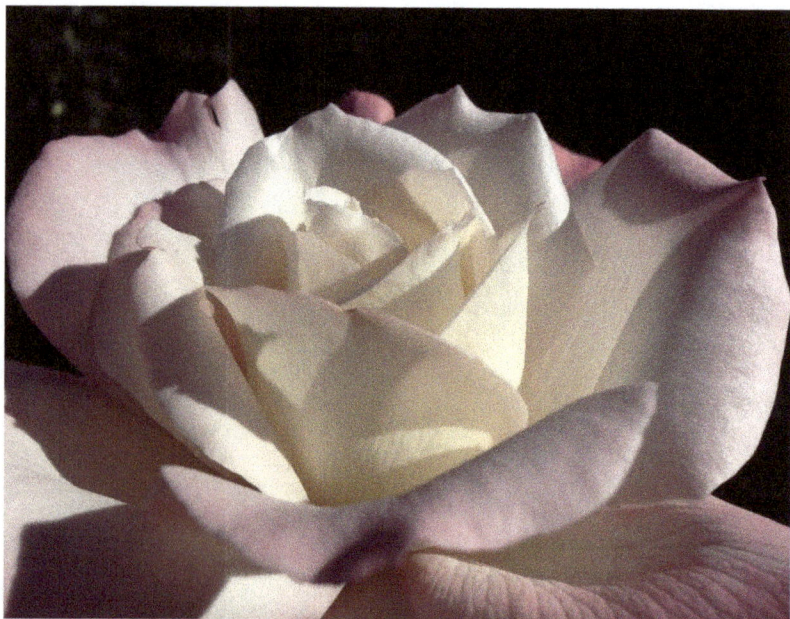

LOVING

ADORATIO

After the Crossing

Imagine Lethe, the river of forgetfulness
just behind you. Its foamy waves,
curling in darkness. You made it.
You did not forget. The Great White
Desert let you pass. It sighed heavily, unwilling.

You are here. Standing under the canopy
of stars in liquid amber sky. Your toes
sink into the carpet of evening grass,
the luxury of ermine smoothness.

You are sheltered by monumental trees,
weighing the ages with cosmic precision.
They remind you of the beak of the toucan,
its multi-colored feathers shining in the mist.

The path's unveiled — birds led you
all the way. You made it. You are here.
You remember. The verdant softness
beckons you to lie down, watch
the rainbow flight of the toucans,
the unfurling wings of dawn's
bright swans.

I'm glad you came. I'm glad we made it.
We are here. We did not forget.

Rose Garland

I thought roses.
I thought rich, velvet blossoms.
I thought a red rainbow
from deep crimson to delicately pinkish.

The secret was underground
where the roots sustain
the multi-hued orgy of sensuous allure –
flowers opening to dazzle and fade.

The strength of the rose
is invisible – you see the blush
of seduction in each leaf and petal,

You admire their charms.
Yet, you care for what's out of sight,
not for the obvious.

I thought your love.
I thought how you adore me.
I went deeper down to the source.

The rose, Sappho's lightning
of beauty, breathes love,
laughs at the wind and wonders.

The mystic rosebush dances,
crowned with the royal
garland of fire.

Vortex

You take me
beyond the beginning
into a country
uniquely of yours

Where waves endlessly crash
on the shore
under the One Love's
gentle whisper –
I clear my head
of everything, but you

I rest safely
you come closer –
I enter into
the galaxies of peace
swirling gently
above your heartbeat

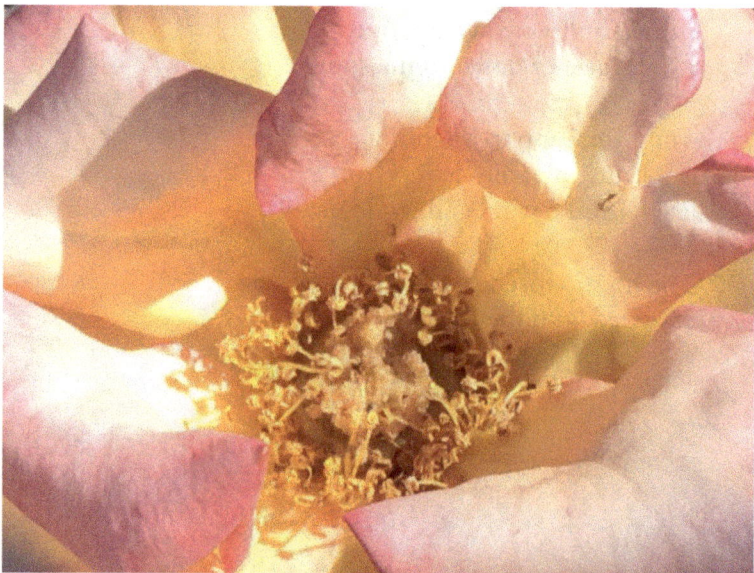

Lauda

It waxes and wanes
with the moon

It grows and recedes with the tides
flowing through my veins
with every heartbeat

It shines in the dark
like phosphorescent letters
on a child's shirt

It is so full of color
that it shames the rainbow
and dims the neon glare
of acrylic wonderland

Indestructible
it has outgrown my despair
my anguish, my pride

Like child's laughter
in an empty room,
like the stillness
of crystal mountain air

Beyond words
love is

Rose Window

I place you in the heart
of my rose, the red one
with dew drops on its leaves.

Like a tricked-up baby
from Ann Geddes' postcard
you rest, snugly wrapped
in the comfort of my love.

"That too shall pass," they say,
"That too shall pass.
The rose will wither,
love will fade away."

Respectfully, I disagree.

I know the symmetry
of velvet petals
is but an opening
into a different universe,
a cosmic window,
timeless.

I see it in the shyness
of your smile. Yes.
You are that lucky.

In the morning
when the curtains of mist
open above silver hills
carved from distance
like a Japanese woodcut,
you taste freedom.

You found your true self
under the detritus
of disordered life.

Isn't it strange
that you've been saved
by the perfection
of just one rose?

Future, Past Perfect

A yellow envelope on my nightstand
shines with a pattern of cursive letters –
"To my sticky Soul Mate."

True, we are stuck together –
for centuries slipping in and out
of time, floating on waves
of amber honey – –as we replay
endless variations of our love story –

You build a house at the edge
of a forest meadow – sunrays
brighten its lace-curtained windows.
I burn my hands weaving a shirt
of nettles to throw on your shoulders
before we succumb to flames.
You ride your chestnut gelding,
with a gift of one scarlet rose,
rushing home after the sunset.
I trip and fall on steep, rocky path, alone.
We swim across a mountain lake –
rainbow ripples scatter on turquoise
surface under our bronzed arms,
moving in twin rhythmic gestures
to reach safety of the other shore.
We lie down on velvet green moss,
under fragrant pine branches
and the twinkling canopy of stars

We meet again and again – a new
variation in topaz and sapphire
has brought us together from beyond
the ocean – will this song last?

Many Happy Returns

Translucent, surrounded by smiley wrinkles, your eyes
shine in brilliant noon light. Your irises of liquid honey
glow with wisdom of centuries, desire that survived
eons of star births and exploding supernovas.

You look at me with helpless affection. I smile.
You do not understand. I do not either.
This certainty – so unanticipated, bewildering,
unexplained. Is it Chance? Destiny? Fate?

Are we reincarnated souls of an Indian maharajah
and his almond-eyed beloved? Did she burn
on the pyre, a widow swathed in scarlet silks
of bridal love? Is that why I am so afraid of fire?

I do not fear heights. I breathe freely. Were we
two wool-clad Incas climbing over rock outcrops
toward condors and dark thunder clouds,
miles above the grassy knoll of the valley?

Was I kidnapped by a fierce blond Viking to share
his awkward kindness? Swallowing my tears
in a wild country of fjords and cliffs; hard land,
chiseled like the contours of your cheeks?

A stranger, I came here from across the ocean.
I left my people, like Ruth in the fields of Boaz.
I gleam my crops alone, after the harvest.
I pick gold nuggets, minutes in your presence

shared afternoons in my garden of sparrows
and orange blossoms. I found you here. We
found each other in this wordless gift – the only
armor against relentless steel of measured time.

Adorable

> … is the word for you.

Yes, you've heard me right.
Like a kitten? More a baby golden lab,
a cuddly puppy with huge chocolate eyes
looking at me with untamed affection.
Excited, impatiently waiting to be hugged.
Adorable – as in the French perfume
"J'adore" – but not the flowery kind.
The musky spice of your naked body.

gentle, shy, hopeful, fit, boisterous, persistent
singing carols out of tune, with muscles flexing
under sun-kissed skin – ready for a home run
nice, not naughty, but nice – through and through

How do I know? The word appeared
while I was driving down the Five
at night, dozing off, stopping for naps,
moving on in a blur of hours, miles,
hills, exit signs and darkness.
I was rushing to be home when you
called. This word floated up
through the fog of exhaustion
in the lunar landscape of bare hills
near Avenal State Prison, marking
the strange topology of your dreams.

sensuous, sweet, exotic, defiant, witty,
bewildering – alive, soo alive –

Yes, you've heard me right.
I've got just one word for you,
for the whole you – *adorable.*

A Jewel Box Sunrise

Silver cirrus clouds float west
like shoals of fish in an amethyst sky.
Sun rises over a wintry orchard.
The smooth zeppelin of poetry
carries me above the tangle of dreams.
I rest, bruised after stumbling
through twisted roots, broken tree limbs.

Frost grows flowers on window panes.
See how they dance? You nod
over your morning tea. "You are welcome"
I smile at your questioning gaze.
My Grandma's gold-rimmed china cup
warms your hands. Steam rises
from the bright topaz liquid.

"Tea flows in your veins, sweets,"
you say, laughing. The helium of words
fills the skin of the moment.
"Come here," you say, wrapping
your arms around my waist.
A kiss of herbal fragrance.
Dawn blossoms into lucid light.

We go outside, stand under
snow-covered cherry trees.
They sigh and crackle. Their sap
rises deep beneath the bark.

The white balloons of our breath
dissipate through cold air crystals.
Having waited so long, I'm glad
for my jewel box sunrise.

Always

The voice of Patsy Cline
hovers above sweet cuteness of pastels
brightly hued like the Polish candy
we call *landrynki* and laugh
when the sugar dye paints
our tongues with fake pink and blue
fuchsia and lavender

We walk down the country road
to our pink and blue homes,
in a fuchsia and lavender embrace
under matching, happy hills that sing

I'll be loving you, always
With the love that's true, always

Countryside

Years add up. We drive through
countryside singed by summer,
plants exhausted by sunlight,
bringing forth fruit. You hold
the steering wheel. Your bald spot
is showing when you lean forward
intent on seeing the road ahead.

I smile and caress your cheek.
I'm glad you saw me that day.
You watched my hips move
with each step, breasts heaving
when I could not catch my dog.
He came to you and so did I.
You caught yourself a prize.

Now it is my turn to care for you
in your weariness. I'll spread
the blanket of my love
over your hunched shoulders.
Your sorrow will evaporate
under my tender touch.

Today, I am Saint Maja
full of compassion
and grace.

On Landscapes: A Guidebook

First you cross the Salt Plains of Rejection
into the Desert of Abandonment.
Mount Disappointment lies just beyond
the Valley of Regret. This is a huge country.
You lived there for decades. You explored
every nook and cranny; path, boulder, crevice.

Ever since your mother disappeared
for five months and a year. Ever since
you learned to write at six to send her
your desperate pleas: "Mommy, come back.
Mommy, I love you. Mommy, why don't you
love me, anymore?" You re-lived this story
time and time again. In every marriage, romance.

Now you know too well how it feels.
Now you can open the enchanted book
and say the words of magic.
You pour out a River of Molten Light –
dazzling, white hot, yet cool to touch –
over the chaff of broken feelings, the dust
of memories you wish were not yours
to keep and gather for the Ancient One.

> *The chaff burns.*
> *The shadows flee.*
> *You find a grain of gold*
> *Under your feet.*
> *Smooth, shiny, polished,*
> *It is yours to keep.*

Is it a grain? Look closer, a golden acorn
rests in the palm of your hand. Plant it
in Guilt Valleys. Plant it in the Deserts
of Despair. Plant on Fear Mountain slopes.

Plant it on wind-swept Plains of Sorrow. It grows so fast.
Soon, a magnificent Oak Tree spreads out its gold leaves
and boughs. New life in your Landscape of Desolation.
Look through its branches. Be mindful, attentive.
What do you see? Here: The Fertile Fields of Bonding.
There: The Rainbow Meadows of Connection.

Look carefully now. See the Pristine Peaks
of Fulfillment, the Sun Gardens of Gratitude?
Filled with every kind of fragrant blossoms,
the heady perfume of rose and jasmine,
the delicate scent of lavender, forget-me-nots,
with liquid melodies of birdsong in the air.

This is not a mirage. This is your own world
to conjure up, delight in.
Here. This gold grain is for you. Will it become
an acorn or a pinecone in your hand?
Come. Let's plant it and watch it grow.

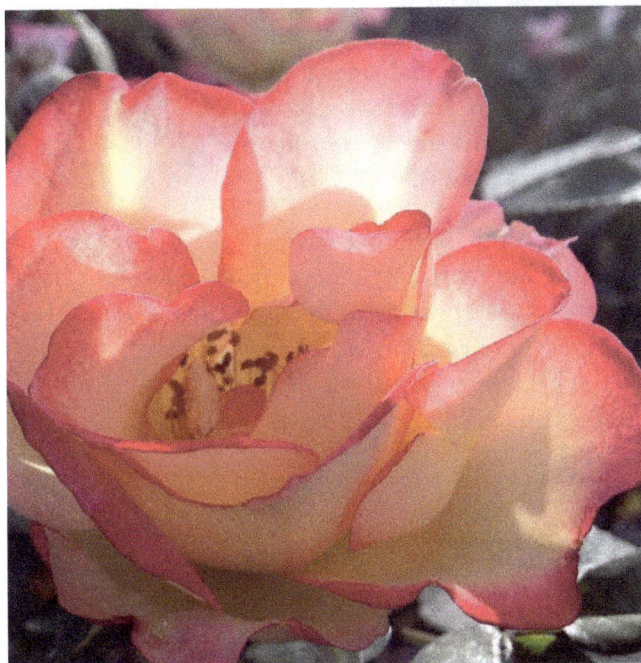

Skylark's Lesson

Don't strive. Don't fight.
Don't go beyond yourself, tensely
stretching, grasping, in an effort
to bend reality to your own will
"I want, I want, I want..."

Listen. Leave this. Relax into Love
surrounding you like the smooth surface
of a mountain lake, rosy at dawn,
reflecting clearly the splendor
of crystalline peaks, glistening
with new snow, in tranquil stillness.

Be glad, so glad. Be calm, so calm. Content.
Breathe deeply. Fill your whole being
with happiness found among white daisies,
fragrant clover and golden dandelions
on a spring meadow, under the bell
of a sky, ringing with pure tones
of a lone skylark that sings away,
up in the azure, among puffy clouds
The sky is mirrored in the softness
of cornflowers and bluebells.

Be still, so still, like a pine forest
at noon, hot with the fullness of summer
treetops barely stirring in the light breeze
whispering to each other, to you
to the birds, weary with sleep after
their extravaganza of the dawn chorus.

"The Sun is up. The Sun is up.
The Sun is everywhere. The Sun
caresses our crowns and we

grow — grow — grow —from deep waters
of the Earth into Sunlight."

Breathe deeply, slowly, deeply.
IN —the tension constricting your heart
with worries of today, yesterday, tomorrow.
OUT — the openness of Love, of loving all,
seeing all, touching all, being all,
flowing freely, brilliantly in waves
of liquid light—within you, around you,
over you — here, now, always, now —

Relax into Love. Be still, so still.
Be glad, so glad, be happy.
Blossom like the Earth's gentle smile,
like the *khorovod* of trees, birds' servants
sustaining all among their leaves and branches.

Is there anything you want to know?

The answer is here already,
waiting for you in the center
of your wide-open heart.

Liquid Honey

Warm, translucent, glowing irises
surrounded by smiley wrinkles,
your eyes look at me
with the wisdom of centuries,
desire that survived all ages
of star births, exploding supernovas.

Translucent with irises
like liquid honey your eyes look
at me in merciless noon light,
clearly outlining each wrinkle
on your forehead, the fruit
of worry, not trusting my love.

Every turn of our walk
through the fragrant chaparral,
scented by manzanita and sage,
is a dance of affection –
every step is a caress.

Love flows through the air to bind us.
I hold your arm, lean my head onto
your shoulder, our hips touch lightly.

I feel the weight of your hand
on my waist, pulling me into the vortex –
the unknown – what has to be –

Topaz Eyes

A magpie, I like all things shiny:
pearls, quartz earrings I wore in New York
at the top of the World Trade Center
before the twin towers fell –

A silver brooch from Polish mountains,
cheap imitation, but lustrous – it counts.
A pink opal from who knows where –
Australian backcountry, maybe –
with a miniature, multicolored light inside.

Iridescent feathers on a peacock's tail
and the halo of goodness around you,
the magic of God's brilliance –
affection sparkling in your topaz eyes.

Things Not to Say on a Lazy Afternoon

You ask me, what am I doing?

I'm taming the wild foxes – everywhere, in you, in me.
Their sharp teeth look better in a smile. They learn
to stop growling, eat cloud berries, not souls.

But what about mice, you say, ever mindful
of the world's balance, adding shadow to every
good deed? Yes, without foxes, our harvest
would have been all gone, devoured.

I'm enchanted with the eerie beauty of foxes.
Their smooth copper fur. White-tipped tails wave
like the flag of surrender. Bright topaz eyes sparkle.
Smart and wary, foxes are always ready to run.

I'm taming the wild foxes – in me, in the world, in you.
Each winsome thought, word, or gesture; each tender
touch of affection gentles them slightly, step by step –

From snarls into smiles – from bristles to giggles
they are calmer, kinder, lovelier – *a bit more* –

*Come closer, let me caress your gold, glossy
coat* – rich and lustrous, the softest to touch.
*Come, you will like it, by my side, lean over
– a bit more – a bit more – a bit more –*

In Case You Did Not Know

Yes, I do love my shape-shifting demon
You know, my dear, I do.

The hungry demon of mischief and pleasure.
The charming demon of seduction and grace.

I let him hear my sweet Polish voice
I let him sense my white diamond scent

I let him feel the warmth of my skin
I hear his heartbeat, so strong and true

Yes, you should know, I do.

How to Domesticate a Cat

A tiger, really, crouching in the corner of your yard
with bared teeth – tired, terrified –

You just sit there, read, sit, don't let him
notice you are watching – the fur so sleek
the play of muscles underneath –
chocolate hazel of his eyes
Sing – no – hum of misty Wonderland,
love that's here to stay, whisper sunshine
into warm air, in receding darkness
under closed eyelids –

– who knows how long I've loved you –

Stretch out your hand and pet him
on the back – pretend you do not notice
how he strains to prolong your touch
with a spark in his eyes – close, right next to you

Somehow, he gets even closer –
Feed him choice morsels off your hand
Tell stories, *sotto voce* – hypnotize him
with exotic melody of an alien language

Oblivious, he will lean into you
warming you with his heartbeat –

– steady – steady – cicho – sza –

Just sit there, burying your fingers
in the blond fur, caressing the silkiness
of his strong, tamed shoulders, that move
rhythmically with your touch.

– closer – closer – cicho – szaa –

This is the dance of togetherness,
a fearless, glorious waltz
of now – only now –

cicho – cicho – cicho – szaaa –

NOTE: *"Cicho" means "quiet" in Polish, "cicho sza" means "there, there" said in English to comfort someone.*

Midnight Cat

This is what you do when you encounter
the Midnight Cat – terrifying, huge, relentless,
overpowering you with his demonic strength.
His paw stretches towards you with enormous,
sharp, black claws, the stuff of horrors.

You gently pat the dark, lustrous fur and say:
"Put those away. You do not need to hurt me.
You are just fine, the way you are…"

A star of Light appears on the smooth coat
under your palm. You touch his ears –
they turn snow white. You kiss his eyes –
now golden, topaz, not fathomless black.

You sit down by his side and rest your head
on his strong chest, listening to the patter
of the beating heart – growing stronger,
more confident, true.

Bright stars appear on his gleaming fur
under your fingertips. The coat of darkness
turns pristine white, sparkling like mountains
on a crisp day in mid-winter.

You think your thoughts that he can hear.
"Expand, expand, forever expand, into
Light, into Love, into Love, into Light" –
You sing songs for your Demon of Night.

Strong, oh so strong, sweet, oh, so sweet.
Powerful, witty, smart, attentive, focused,

creative, lovely, gentle, delightful, surprising,
uncontrollably wild, beyond comprehension,
infinitely graceful, charming, seductive –
the Force of Nature – your Midnight Cat.

You kiss his forehead – that's the last thing
you do. The Mystic Star blooms on his brow,
brilliant in the lucid air all around you.

Are you sorry that his coat becomes the clearest
flawless crystal white, scintillating like stars in the distance?

Light spreads, bright and brighter still, until
you see and are too shy to touch, a luminous diamond
Cat of Divine Light, leaping through rainbows.

Sunfire Foxes

I come from a tribe of nine-tailed foxes.
You are a gold fox with nine tails too.

We splash in the pools of silver moonlight.
We chase bright stars through violet sky.

We catch a ride on a sparkling comet,
Nourished by nectar of honey dew

We leap through sunbursts, sunfire, sunrays.
We rest in the golden glow of noon.

Our wisdom grows in spirals, circles.
Our joy is boundless, our love is true.

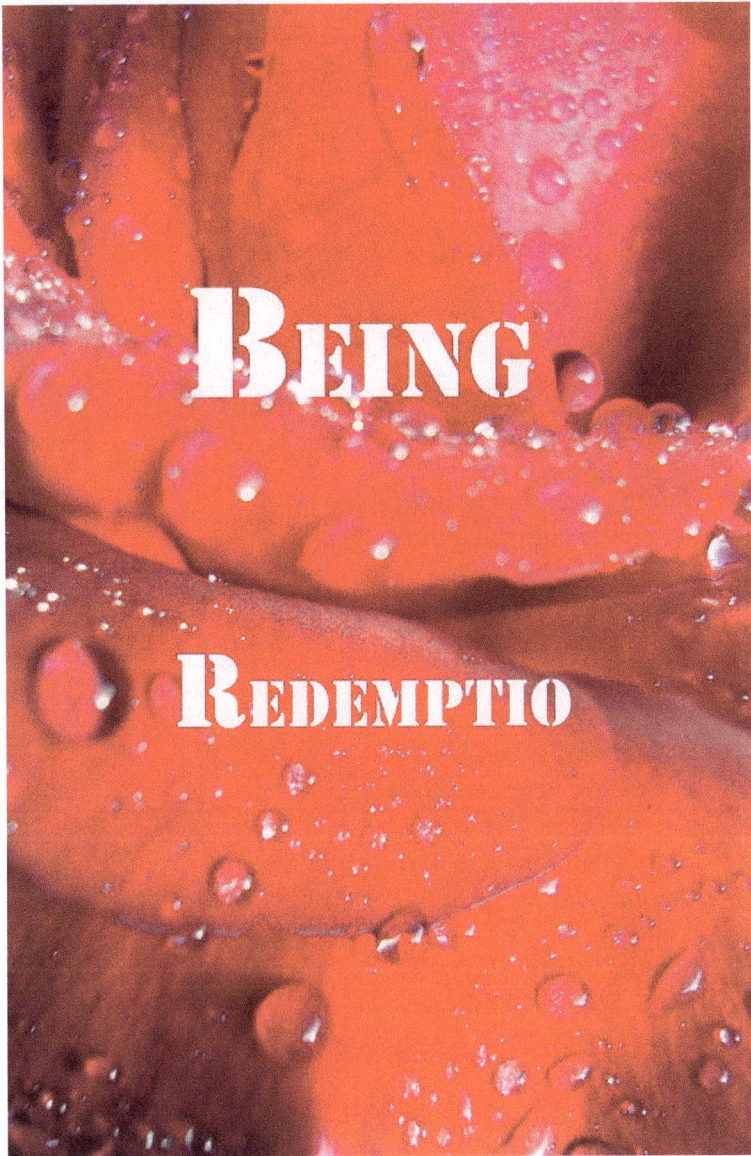

BEING

REDEMPTIO

Lost and Found

... the sky of the sky of a tree called life
~ e.e. cummings

I found myself
in a perfect place

I laugh to tears
and I like what I see

after broken pieces
of Devil's mirror were
washed away from my eyes

There's no torment here,
no limits, only the infinite
glory of becoming One

with Universe, One with
the Divine, stumbling on my way

No anxiety, no desire –
I live right here, right now

Thank you for the key
that opened my door to Paradise –

Serene, fearless, I'm wholly
and whole made of Love –

Diamond Days in Crystal Gardens

... towards the door we never opened, into the rose-garden
~ T.S.Eliot's *Little Gidding*

Once I was a Princess of Shining Flame,
a Rose in the Palace of Fire,
searching for my Knight of Lightning,
my Prince of the Sun Chariot.

I looked and looked, in one country, the next.
I even crossed the ocean, lured by the siren call
of the unknown, enchanted by its blissful promise.

I will not tell you what I found and discarded,
time and time again – like Doc in the diamond mine,
throwing away jewels of dark hues, listening for flaws
in their voices. I left behind what was no longer needed,
even pity that I wished for these things at all.

Now, I'm the Queen of the Throne of Violet Flame;
the Empress of Contentment. I find untold treasures
in my garden, sheltered by seven hills and dales,
protected by blue agave and thorns of my roses.

Emerald tree leaves glow under sapphire cupola.
Diamond dew drops cover my lawn
with a fortune of good wishes.

From dawn to dusk, hummingbirds, finches
and doves fill the air with the flutter of wings,
fluted arabesques of their calls. They rest at noon
for a moment of awe at the Majesty, the Sun.

I rest here, too, caressed by the breeze,
scented by orange blossoms, mint, and jasmine.
I drink from the clear streams of living waters.

I pick bunches of wildflowers from sun-drenched meadows
– red poppies, sun-like daisies, blue stars of cornflowers
and forget-me-nots, all wrapped in green lace of forest fern.

I give away rich bouquets of velvet roses – burgundy, gold
and alba, with shades of mauve, peach, and vermillion.
Would you like a bouquet like that?

I am the Empress of Contentment. My realm stretches
as far as I can see: to the horizon of Pacific Ocean
shimmering in the summer heat, bringing the homage
of wave after wave to my sandy toes.

Sometimes, I find seashells, with an endless melody within,
reaching to the distant galaxies of midnight heavens.

I glow brighter than the brightest star. I'm a rainbow
of infinite radiance. All made of Love, I'm the fountain
of Living Light, a droplet in the wave of Cosmic Ocean.

See the Sea

Hi, sweet dolphin
do you want to frolic
in the salty waves of endless ocean?
Feel the smoothness, liquid caress
silky warmth all over you?

Oh, the grace, the light —
noon's lucid fire!

> *— currents in the sea —*
> *— rivers in the ocean —*

Two dolphins
dancing on the waves
we drift through constellations
into One song

We splash in the mist of
cosmic sea foam

From murky depths, we rise
to breathe in translucent sunlight

Together, we ascend
above beds of coral
swirling through spirals
of amber and aquamarine

Radiant, serene
we float on incandescent air
carrying us into
the Cloud of Unknowing

Imagine – A Poem of Light

… a cloud that scatters pearls
~ Rumi

Are you an apple? Or perhaps
a ripe seed inside an apple of light?
You are snug and safe in the core of a torus
of light rays. You are wrapped in white
silk of light. Rays come from your crown into
toes, surrounding you with a bright cocoon,
of magnetic lines. Six winged angels stand
on all sides, watching over you.

No angels? Are you a fountain, then?
Your heart – the spring of goodness.
Liquid light overflows from within you.
Your heartbeat marks the smooth rhythm,
the gentle pulse of the sky of the sky of the sky.
The light! This miracle you forget about
every day as your blood carries your
heart-light into every cell of your body.

Not a fountain? A star, perchance?
Or, maybe, two stars. A large one brightly shines
on your chest, its rays straight and dazzling.
Multicolored sparkles dance in the brightness
of your aura. See, the second star blossoms
right above you, as radiant as the heart star?

Here you are: an arc between stars,
a lucid rainbow of ancient gold
still shining, shining, shining –

On Divine Comedy and Ice-Cream

My Muse has topaz eyes and a goatee.
Disabled by grief, he looks for me in the dark,
touching. His hands outline the contour
of my hips as he sighs and says "that's right"
in this deep baritone of his, the sweetest of voices.

What next? I wonder as we sit on leather sofa
sticky in the heat – eat almonds and ice cream
with milk – watch silly comedies about aliens
and time machines, friends playing air guitar
being excellent to each other.

We leaf through the other Comedy, the Divine –
Dante's *Il Paradiso* in visions by Giovanni di Paolo –
medieval illuminations for the end of time.

Submerged in Earth's shadow, the Moon sphere
is the haven for the likes of us, inconstant,
waxing and waning, not keeping their vows.
Dante and Beatrix, the poet and his beloved,
rise up to Mercury of the ambitious and Venus
of lovers, to the Garden of Earthly Delights where
we stay, as they ascend from the Fourth Sphere
of the Sun through the Eighth of Fixed Stars.
In Primum Mobile, they meet the wise and virtuous,
martyrs and saints, with a multitude of angels
and the blessed, don't forget the blessed
of the Tenth Sphere, Divine Empyrean –

the heart of Paradise where gold rays of Light
always permeate everything, where saints
sleep in rose petal pods, tranquil like babies

by their mothers – or joyously splash in and out
of the waters of grace, the river of serenity
that flows under the buzzing of heavenly bees,
making timeless honey – sweet, translucent
gold honey, only honey –
forever and beyond time
honey —

Revelation after *Il Paradiso*

We live in the Third Sphere
of lovers, in Earth's long shadow.
Our love waxes and wanes
like the Moon, or Venus rising up
before dawn, the Star of Morning.

We oscillate from darkness to brilliance,
float from opaque fear into sunlight
to rest on a golden afternoon
in the innocent warmth of affection
among newly planted roses –
Imperial, Fireglow, Compassion,
Double Delight and Simplicity roses
in our garden where we trim twisted
branches of old oleanders to make room
for oranges and more pomegranate –
always more pomegranate –
never enough pomegranate –

Dark-red, translucent juice stains
our fingers – tart fruit bursts with flavor
in our mouths, ready for kisses
always ready for more kisses –
softest, childlike, strongest, tasting
like wine we never tasted – dreams
we never even hoped to dream
about escaping the long shadow
of Earth on a golden afternoon –

Lovers in the Garden of Love
resting in the Third Sphere of Venus –
Golden, golden, sparkling golden
afternoon on another planet –

Gold, Inside

You say –
"My heart beats for you"

You write
about your "ear-to-ear smile"

You ask
"Will you be mine?"

You know the answer
hidden in plain sight –

it blossoms
in my garden

* * *

come –
unlock
its secret

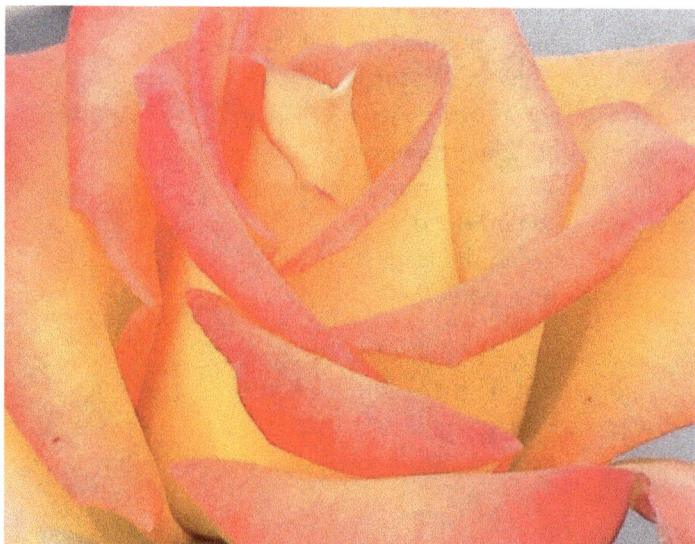

Sweet Nothings

We are the wings of a butterfly
Dancing in the vortex of time
Ascending to the heart of the galaxy
Flying higher and higher and higher

> *I love you. You love me.*
> *I love you. You love me.*
> *We are love, love, love, love*
> *One love.*

We are the wings of the butterfly
Twirling with a flutter in the breeze of time
Carried by currents beyond what's known
We swirl and rise up, together

> *I love you. You love me.*
> *We are love.*

What remains of the wings torn apart?
Is the pattern eternal? Does it stay
Once created and outlined in pure light,
embroidered on the fabric of reality
with a sparkling golden thread of memory?

> *Yes, I love you. You love me.*
> *I love you. You love me.*
> *We are love, love, love, love*
> *True love.*

An Invitation to the Dance

And the angels are dancing.
Did you say dancing? Yes, dancing. Making somersaults
and jumping two hundred yards in the air.

Air? Are they here? I thought they lived in infinity,
or eternity, or the great beyond, or whatchamacallit.
No. Here. They are laughing their heads off. Giggling,
smiling, smirking, guffawing. Laughing.

What's so funny? Nic. Nada. Naught. It is just that they are
so happy. So incredibly, exorbitantly, blissfully happy.

Why? Oh, because of that quirky thing
from the country song.

What thing? Don't you know? Have you not heard
that love conquers all? That love triumphs
over lies, fear, anger, shame and despair?
That it is? Love is. True love. Our love…

It blossoms in us, through us.
It opens its petals. The world is more tranquil,
serene in the luminescence of our love.
New stars are born. Cherries are sweeter when we
are together, immersed in this love. When we
find it. Return to it. Share it. Cherish it. When we
are not giving up. No matter what. No matter how hard.
No matter how late. It is soo simple, very simple.
Impossible? Yet, it is here to stay.

So, what about these angels, then…

Oh, yes. Would you like to go dancing with angels?
Boogie-woogie, waltz, tango or salsa?

I Did Not Dare to Hope

Yet I know it is true.
This certainty is of a bubbly
sparkling kind – it floats up
like champagne in a tall flute
to welcome the New Year
of promises to keep, of bliss-filled
Love that never was, but always is –
always as in a country song of old
shining on pink rose petals
covered with diamond dew
in the morning, under
the periwinkle skies
"of endless possibilities
and our greatest dreams"
that we've known
and will know –
together.

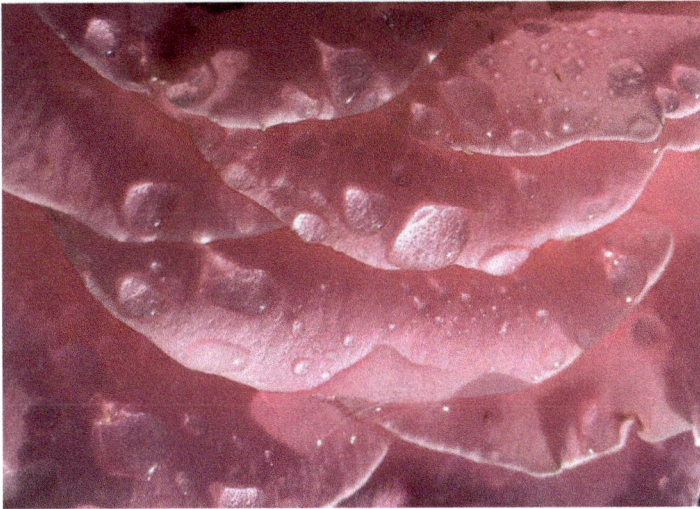

What I Learned on Friday Morning

A letter.
A letter in cursive.
A letter in my mailbox
by the evergreen bush, full of sparrows.

Old-fashioned joy of holding paper in my hands,
thinking of the moment when ink touched the surface,
feelings became signs to be deciphered.

Joy.
Radiant joy.
Joy that glows, though you
cannot see it through tears, it is more
real than the flash of fright, your heart sinking,
Stronger than the sudden pang of pain awoken
by unwanted memory, lingering for decades.

First, do no harm.
First, plant a fragrant flower –
sweet alyssum, baby's breath.
First, breathe deeply.

Breathing.
At one with the world.
Reaching for peace – shredded
by the shrieks of crows that gather for
their dark feast on the half-dead oak by dry riverbed.

"No hatred, no resentment, not even a slight dislike" –
said the saint whom the world doesn't know, will not know,
blinded by rage, blooming endlessly in fear and isolation.

Circles.
Radiant circles.
Circles of compassion open
blossom, link and sing the elemental
rainbow into being – all colors into one vibrant light.

As above, so below. The flower of life
spreads its petals through galaxies, seeds an infinity
of planets into beauty, blooming gloriously in the storm.

I am you and you and you – we are one –
Love and Light – the circle and the ray –
the wave of particles holds us –
united – unfolding –
true –

Winter Solstice

Remember –
I'm not your girlfriend
I am your interstellar wife
You, my interstellar husband

We meet
in clouds above clouds
beyond violet sunrise –

Hand in hand, we float
into infinity

We hold
paired spheres
of brightly polished copper
and glowing amber
smooth as honey –
for harmony and balance
of body and soul

We become
stronger, more aware
each day

Affection
explodes into twin flames
dancing through galaxies
tightly intertwined —
round and round, beyond

Ascending
into crystalline whiteness
above star orchards

we pass through
fragrant blizzards
swirling dogwood petals
cherry blossoms

Crowned
with timeless jewels
we are the most serene
prince and princess
of interstellar flight

Midnight Sun

In the rain of sweat droplets
I found laughter – bubbling from my lips
rediscovered under the diamond sun
in iridescent, crystal sky

You laugh, too – innocent –
light-hearted – when my hands
meet at the nape of your neck
and slide down in a game
of childish delight

You say – The *fire is alive in my soul*
This comes from deep within
My heart is opening to your love

Golden contours of your body
glow with grace from within

Crowned with the rose
of a thousand petals
I'm a bright star of midnight –
radiant with joy

Life's river flows through me –
awakens a secret song
I have forgotten

Twin flames – lost, long sought
found and found again –
we are an ascending spiral
of Light – sparkling, twirling
in an ancient dance –

– *ever-present, always, now* –

High Noon

Forever – is made of Nows
~ Emily Dickinson

All silent, we wait with bated breath
for the next word from the Great Sun –
a life changing utterance of grace and might.

Everything drinks in the brilliance
in this land of butterflies and jasmine,
as birds doze off, hidden in tree branches,
while radiant light caresses our backs.

We fall asleep, drunk on luminosity,
lightness tightly wrapped in soft feathers,
overshadowed by smooth cherub wings.

It is so quiet now, at the high noon of summer.
Satiated, tranquil, we dream in the bright arms
of the Sun. Our DNA codes are cleared and sorted.

Our cells sparkle, permeated with liquid light.
Photons trickle into every twist of the
Double helix. There is no absence, need,
want or sorrow. All is bliss – all peace –
all perfection – now – just now – right now –

Just to Make It Clear

Two falling stars in the day sky
~Hafiz

A woman is a sunburst shining in darkness.
A man is a sunray piercing the clouds.

The arrow flows straight into the heart of intention.
The wave envelops the world with pure Love.

Like a photon of Light – a particle, smooth wave –
the two become One, the mystery Divine.

A woman, a man, two faces of brightness.
The radiance of starlight, so dazzling as One.

They blossom on petals of pure Divine Fire.
They float on unfolding wings of Divine Flame.

A woman, a man. Love's only desire.
Light's pure revelation – a true cosmic gem.

Last Pomegranate

I ate it this morning. It looked abandoned
on the bare branch, a twig really,
too weak to support the ripe fruit.
And yet, here it was – after heavy rains,
frost, winter storms.

Arils shone like a handful of rubies
on my palm, sparkling in bright sunlight
under the azure sky, so clear this Sunday,
this day of YES.

The taste – intensely sweet, delightful –
carmine juice spilling on my fingers –
seeds getting stuck in my teeth.

"My sticky Soul Mate" – you wrote once.
A yellow envelope sat on my bedside cabinet
for a long time, far too long. I could not part
with this witty admission of being stuck
to each other, even when other letters
were burnt, confined to flames.

"You are my sticky Soul Mate" – refreshing
like the scarlet droplets of last pomegranate
bursting with tart sweetness, clearing
my mind and calming my body
into certainty, with a tender assurance
that all is well, and all shall be well
for we are One, in this Knowing.

My Birthday Gift

••• came in an envelope, written
in cursive, a flowing, elegant script.

When you wake up on your Birthday,
walk outside and may the Sun reach down
and kiss you. This is my Birthday wish for you.

If you ever decided to give me a chance to redeem
my Love for you in this lifetime, I know in my heart
that I would love you and only you like you never knew.
My Birthday and my lifetime gift to you is **me.**
Yea. All of me. My Heart, Mind, Body and Soul.

Know this, I will never be apologetic claiming
my Love for you!!!

Thank you for saving me from me. I get
so lost in this world and you are the only one
who has ever reached me, you are always
lifting me up. No one has, or ever will, be
as special to me as you. You are my world
today, tomorrow and forever!!!

I can't wait to share my true love for you –
By caring for you, being kind and gentle,
always putting you first, being honest and
compassionate and always by your side.
I am waking up in my life to see True Love.

I am going to love you, like no one has
loved you. You are always the miracle
that makes my life complete, and I will do
everything I can to make your life so sweet.

I am set, for decades to come, renewing my love
for you. We will thrive, making our own destiny.

Life in itself will be much more worth living for,
being by your side. Our bodies soaking up
every sunset, the Sun will shine ever brighter.

I have been touched by an Angel, that is you!
It is time for the Angel to come out in me,
returning the Love, touching you.

All I want is to live in Love, in Love with you.
Side by side, walking through this life.

Will you walk by my side?

Twin Flame Promise

to have, to hold, and to cherish
~ old English wedding vows

I take you to be my beloved
for today and tomorrow
for all days and nights
for a week and all weeks
for a month and all months
for a year and all years
for all eternity
wherever we are and will be
in rain and sunlight
in joy and happy togetherness
of our most holy marriage
our divine union

I promise you solemnly my love
faithfulness and honesty
and that I will not leave you until my death
I will be with you as long as I exist
I promise you the love of my heart
because you are my heart –
and the love of my body
because you are my body –
and the love of my eyes
because you are the light of my eyes –
and the love of my soul
because you are my soul mate
my being's other half
my fulfilment now and forever

In God, our Divine Source, Way and Life
sharing our love for ever and ever

And so, let it grow and last and be
my promise for you and yours for me

Late Pomegranates

– are hard to crack open, with rough
dry rinds, yet they taste so sweet,
the sweetest in sunlight on the day
I realize you gave me your blood.
Every drop of the blood in your veins
is now mine, the gift for my birthday.

No screeching of crows will change
that undisputable fact: all the blood
in your veins is mine – you are mine
now and always and always and always –

Such an extravagant, overwhelmingly
generous Gift of Gifts. Of course,
I accept. Time does not matter.
You were mine before we first talked,
could not stop, knowing each other
so well, too well, before we were born
into this life of the hardest test,
the nadir, the truth, and the rebirth.

All is known. There is nothing to say.
I sing my sweet nothings:
I love you, you love me,
we are Love,
Love, Love, Love,
all Love.

In the Valley of Yes

I wrote it out in a thousand words
again, and again, affirming
the forgotten truth.

You opened your eyes, bewildered,
finally seeing what is to be seen,
saying what is to be said:

*We have crossed over into the Soul
now merging into what's before us.*

*That is you on the interior, lining
the depth of my heart. You are the center
of my Universe, as we are aligned
perfectly under the Sun.*

A rarity found true. You and I.

*As we climb the path of life alongside
each other, I am honored to walk with you.*

*Now, I am looking through the lens of Love
that opens into the landscape of you,
a wildflower that comes alive in me.*

*I found a slice of Heaven, in front of me.
It is you! I love you today,
tomorrow and
forever*

Land of Milk and Honey

Kocham Cię, Kochanie Moje.….
I love you, my sweetheart, my love…

in the Sun, crowned by light
in darkness of Moon shadows

as I listen to your voice
deeply resonant, rich, seductive
and sweet like honey

milk and honey, pure honey
of your eyes, warm honey
of your tongue, sweet milk
of our lovemaking
dripping on me all over –

milk and honey of our kisses
the soft, fluid sweetness
of your caress –

silky, smooth
intoxicating

golden heat
of blazing Sun

our Sun –
our Love –
my Love –

Moje Kochanie…

The Heart

...petal by petal, the flower of our heart
~ Amy Lowell

drawing together
the vine of heart leaves
stroke by stroke
from darkness
into light
intertwined –
with the vine
of love

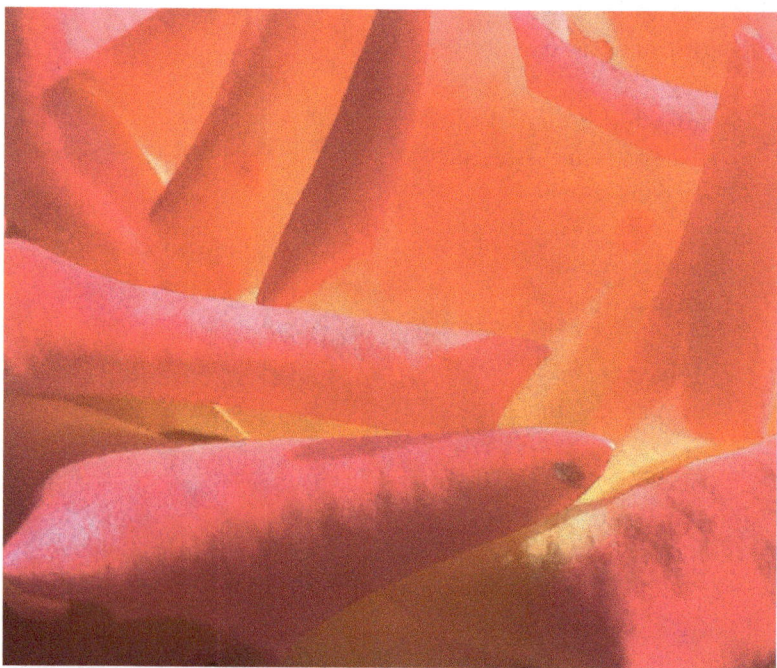

A Day Trip to Venice

The stunt kite traces the infinity sign
over and over above our heads in June-gloom sky
until it twirls into a spiral nose-dive and hits the sand
so hard it falls apart.

Again, it floats up – patiently, gently,
like wings of the dove, so steady high above us, we
float up with the kite into the lucid, pearly milkiness
of clouds, shifting shapes on this strange afternoon.

A lone sailboat disappears into the distance.
Pacific Ocean is cut in half by a sharply outlined pathway
of light leading towards the steely white sun – so hard, so
relentless
it pierces through the mist, carried onshore by steady winds.

We watch the stunt kite dance its dangerous dance.
Ominous steel waves turn into lead. Darkness falls
around us until we cannot see, only feel the tug of the
outstretched lines that keep the kite balanced in the air.

This is the trick of living well, this balance,
staying afloat on marine air currents
lifting us above – higher and higher
into pristine clarity – to postpone
the inevitable crash, avoid
the death spiral at all costs,
any cost – live here and now
in the sweet bye and bye –
forever –

This Afternoon

You are the music while the music lasts.
~ T.S. Eliot, *Little Gidding*

The woodpecker measures time by the thickness
of tree trunks. Birds make nests, hidden from
hawks, safe from scrub jays. We wake in sunlight,
with twirling patterns still under our closed eyelids.

We listen to high-pitched calls of hummingbirds,
the random flutter of wings. We breathe in spring
air, with smoothly flowing melodies of birdsong,
the sweetest of nectars. Waves crash on distant shores
of the Pacific. Stars appear dimly above the horizon,
glowing with the bronzed orange of departing Sun.

We live on the planet of children's laughter.
We watch refractions of light in my sapphire ring,
on diamond dew drops that cling to blades of grass,
half-opened roses. We live on Earth of abundance
and beauty. We live on Earth of plenitude and calm.

There are no sorrows here, no worries.
No before, nor after. No plans. We take deep
breaths, count to eight, inhaling smiles to the tips
of our fingers, into our toes. I laugh. You laugh.
Crystalline peals echo through the Universe –
from galaxy to galaxy, star to star.

We grow and grow – infinite, gentler, wiser –
we understand all, embrace all, know all.
Perfection. Presence. Light.

In the Sweet Bye and Bye

The Tiger came to me for the last time.
Farewell! His broad, rough tongue
licked a streak through the center
of my body. Flexing muscles played
under the skin as he rubbed his side
against my hip. His golden eyes shone
sun-bright, translucent like linden honey
from my Grandma's tree, on a hot July day –
lipiec, full of the healing murmur of bees.

I caressed his smooth coat. My Tiger-Cat –
larger than Life – greater than Legend –
kinder than Justice of the Law of Love.

I let him go.

Yes, I'll see him again. He is always
with me. Forever mine. The other half
of my soul. Lost on twisted pathways.
Found in a flash of recognition –
in a glimpse of shared past – an insight
into the future – our infinite maybe –
One – True – Love – Always – Now –

There were no regrets, no guilt, no shame.
Just this immense wave of relief, mixed in
with the sweetness of gratitude and
the milky warmth of loving kindness.
Two open hearts touching, at last.

It is done, we thought –
We are clear –
We are ready –
We are free –

Amber

Red gold of falling leaves
and amber, liquid amber
engulf me with the intensity
of our love for all seasons –
Even the invisible California winter
without snow, with bright sunshine
and birdsong each morning – in time
for Darjeeling tea, Columbian coffee
and *naleśniki*, flat Polish pancakes
with a touch of maple syrup from Vermont.
The whole world celebrates with us
for we know true meaning of attachment –
not the pink blush of infatuation –
not the wine-red rose of passion –
but this, only this – pure clarity
of azure skies – clear radiance of red gold
and amber – liquid amber

Sapphire

My tiger orchid blooms again
for the third time already

It looks at me shyly
with topaz eyes

thinking, I'd remember
that night, that music
of togetherness –

*Expand, expand, forever
expand* – our hearts fill

with Cosmic Light of
a thousand Suns –

liquid and flowing
to heal and purify

We thank, we praise
the One Love

that blossoms
in emerald gardens

in sapphire flames
and bright tiger eyes

Rainbows

Let's conjure up a lovelier, brighter rainbow
made of jewels, translucent and opaque –

They are you, head to toe, a rainbow "you"
of strength and insight, presence and delight

You are a rainbow of endless Light
You are a fountain of boundless Love

You are a red ruby of life
You are a pure amber of creation
You are a bright gold of strength
You are a green emerald of affection
You are a blue sapphire of truth
You are a clear amethyst of perception

You are a white diamond of light
You are a bright diamond of light

The jewel rainbow of your body
The jewel rainbow of your mind

Grounded in the earth,
reaching for the sky
dancing among stars

you are Love – you are Light

with me

Diamonds

In a seashell there is an ocean
There is Universe within my heart
A myriad galaxies dance in my mind
I'm a microcosm of Divine design

In a seashell there is an ocean
In dark coal mine bright diamonds grow
In your eyes I find ageless wisdom
The One Love that sustains us all

In your guilt I see my darkness
In your beauty – radiance and light
In your voice – the calling, the calling

Mountain air on a spring morning
Sparkling diamonds, radiant and pure –
For all forevers you enfold me in Love

Our Champagne Sunday

Moonlight. Sunlight.
Moonlight breeze. Upside down
half-moon in soft blue sky above us.

It is already four p.m., yet so bright on the
smooth, broad expanse of the beach in Oxnard –
bright and sparkly as if the whole world were champagne.

We hold hands, jump in the waves,
of the Pacific – coming - coming - coming at us
with sprays of sea foam, salty bitterness of long-gone tears,
that will not return. I swear, they will not.

Each wave turns into a burst
of chilled, refreshing bubbly enveloping us
in sudden saltiness – stronger than the jolt of your sweat
dripping onto my lips last night, in our love's endless ocean.

The seawater shines with the translucent
aquamarine perfection of motion – motion – motion.
We float and twirl as effervescent bursts of laughter
flow smoothly, easily off our lips, that know each other
so well, that have known each other for years, ages even.

A full-hearted, full-throated laugh.
Of moonlight. Of sunlight. Of moonlight
breeze. Upside down half-moon
in rich blue sky above us.

The End

Appendix

German music terms

immer langsam – always slow, *sehr klagend* – very plaintively
noch lieblich – still tenderly
Heiliger Dankgesang – "Holy Song of Thanksgiving," the slow movement in
Beethoven's String Quartet Op. 132 in A minor

French terms

joie de vivre – joy of living, *élan vital* – vital force (Henri Bergson)

Italian music terms

accelerando – accelerating
affettuoso – with affection, tenderly
agitato – agitated, fast and excited
colla voce – with the voice
con amore – with love
con brio – with spirit
con fuoco – with fire
con felicità – with happiness
con gioia – with joy
con moto – with motion, lively
da capo – from the beginning
dolce – sweetly
dolcissimo – the sweetest
dolcezza – sweetness
grazioso – gracefully *misterioso* – mysteriously
molto scherzando – very playfully
pianissimo – very soft
più mosso – more
rallentando – decelerating
rubato – in flexibly flowing rhythm
semplicemente – simply
subito – suddenly
sforzando – strained, sharply accented
sotto – subdued
tenderezza – tenderness, softness
tenuto – sustained, holding a single note

About the Author

Maja Trochimczyk, Ph.D., is a Polish American poet, music historian, photographer, and author of seven books on music, most recently *Górecki in Context: Essays on Music* (2017), and *Frédéric Chopin: A Research and Information Guide* (2015). Trochimczyk's eight books of poetry include *Miriam's Iris, Slicing the Bread, The Rainy Bread, Into Light* and three anthologies, *Chopin with Cherries, Meditations on Divine Names,* and *Grateful Conversations*. A former Poet Laureate of Sunland-Tujunga, she is the founder of Moonrise Press and President of the California State Poetry Society. Hundreds of her poems, studies, articles and book chapters appeared in English, Polish, and in many translations in Poland, Canada, U.K., U.S., France, Germany, Sweden, Serbia, China, and other countries. She read papers at over 90 international conferences and is a recipient of honors and awards from Polish, Canadian, and American institutions, such as the American Council of Learned Societies, the Polish Ministry of Culture, PAHA, McGill University, and the University of Southern California. www.trochimczyk.net, poetrylaurels.blogspot.com

www.ingramcontent.com/pod-product-compliance
Lightning Source LLC
Chambersburg PA
CBHW060317100426
42812CB00003B/802